FRETBOARD MASTERY

BY
TROY STETINA

ISBN-13: 978-0-7935-9789-5
ISBN-10: 0-7935-9789-7

HAL•LEONARD®
CORPORATION
7777 W. BLUEMOUND RD. P.O. BOX 13819 MILWAUKEE, WI 53213

Visit Hal Leonard Online at
www.halleonard.com

CONTENTS

Part III: The Structure of Music   44

Part IV: Fusing the Fretboard   89

Part V: Advanced Concepts   116

Appendix   135

About the Author

Troy Stetina is an internationally recognized guitar virtuoso and music educator with more than thirty methods, books, videos, and DVDs published by Hal Leonard Corporation. He is also guitarist for the alternative rock band "Second Soul" and side project "Secret Society of Starfish" on Unicorn Records, plus columnist for *GuitarOne* magazine's "Return of the Shred." Visit him online at *www.stetina.com* for free tips and lessons, plus masterclasses, music CDs, and more.

DVD & Video Methods:
Modern Rock Guitar Signature Licks (DVD)
Hard Rock Guitar Signature Licks (DVD)
Beginning Rock Lead Guitar (DVD & video)
Beginning Rock Rhythm Guitar (DVD & video)
Black Sabbath Signature Licks (DVD)

Books & Book/CD Methods:
Very Best of Ozzy Osbourne Signature Licks (book/CD)
Best of Black Sabbath Signature Licks (book/CD)
Deep Purple Greatest Hits Signature Licks (book/CD)
Aggro-Metal Signature Licks (book/CD)
Total Rock Guitar (book/CD)
Best of Foo Fighters Signature Licks (book/CD)
Rage Against the Machine Signature Licks (book/CD)
Barre Chords – The Ultimate Guide (pocket guide book)
The Ultimate Scale Book (pocket guide book)
Troy Stetina's Guitar Lessons: Hard Rock (book/CD)
Troy Stetina's Guitar Lessons: Funk Rock (book/CD)
Left Handed Guitar – The Complete Method (book/CD)
Beginning Rock Lead Guitar (companion book)
Beginning Rock Rhythm Guitar (companion book)
Metal Lead Guitar Volume 1 – revised (book/CD)
Metal Lead Guitar Volume 2 – revised (book/CD)
Metal Rhythm Guitar Volume 1 – revised (book/CD)
Metal Rhythm Guitar Volume 2 – revised (book/CD)
Metal Lead Guitar Primer (book/CD)
Thrash Guitar Method (book/CD)
Speed Mechanics for Lead Guitar (book/CD)
Heavy Metal Guitar Tricks (book/CD)

Music CDs:
Exottica
Set the World on Fire

Preface

Fretboard Mastery is the natural companion to my advanced technique book, *Speed Mechanics for Lead Guitar*. Both are the result of my personal search as a guitarist.

Years ago my goals on the guitar were essentially two-fold. First, I wanted to eliminate any physical restrictions. That is, I wanted to be able to play anything, including any sequence of notes, at any speed. My experience in developing that kind of technique was then organized into *Speed Mechanics for Lead Guitar* to help others accomplish the same thing. Second, I wanted to understand the fretboard inside and out. I wanted to make it completely transparent, so my ideas could flow instantly from imagination to the guitar without any need to "translate" (i.e., hunt for the right notes). When I heard something, whether from inside or outside my own head, I would know instantly how it appeared. So I could just "think" the fretboard and compose songs and solos entirely in my head. Nice and practical.

However, my pursuit to understand the fretboard didn't stop with the fretboard. How could it? After all, what is the fretboard but the guitarist's gateway into the musical labyrinth? So in order to truly understand and make full use of the fretboard, one must understand music itself. And that brings up my third goal. Did I say I only had two? Never believe that. From early on, I was curious about how music worked in a larger sense. How did my chosen style relate to other styles? What were the common elements and the differences? I sought a unifying view. I wanted to see the big picture as well as my own specialized niche to, I suppose, properly "place" my experience.

The good news is that gradually I achieved this fretboard "transparency" as well as the wider knowledge of music that went with it. As a result, music seems simple. And it is, when you look deeply enough and separate the decorative elements from the meat of it. But make no mistake, it is a simplicity born from a myriad of details and ingrained skills. So it only feels simple after you know it! Not much consolation, I suppose. Nonetheless, this book is my attempt to make it "simple" for you, too.

Fretboard Mastery is a comprehensive ear-training, theory, chord, scale, melody, and soloing book. It builds a powerful yet flexible framework for understanding music and guitar—my view essentially. We start with the very bedrock of sound and build up the structure right to the top, which will allow you to quickly absorb anything you choose and take your music further.

I know that music lives in your untapped imagination, and this book will help you unlock it. Yes, it's advanced. It may at times seem difficult, but persevere. The rewards are more than satisfying and will last a lifetime. Good luck with your playing!

—Troy Stetina

The Goal of *Fretboard Mastery*

Fretboard Mastery is a set of tools designed to make the entire fretboard your playground. Yes, it is challenging. It is intended for intermediate to advanced players who want to see further and take their musicianship to the highest levels. It's not for everyone.

We begin with a long series of ear-training exercises to build the connection between your inner ear and the fretboard. Then we cover a number of the larger musical structures in the primary positions and continue ear-training to recognize them instantly by their sound and associated fretboard shapes. Next we look at how music actually works with regard to tonality, chord progressions, melody, etc. Finally we extend our knowledge over the entire fretboard in a series of superimposed patterns. Through this whole procedure, you learn more than a bunch of scale dot patterns—you learn how to really *use* these various sets of notes to make music. All keys, all scales, all notes, all options.

How is my approach different? Well, let's examine the more common approach. Usually you find such things as scales, chords, arpeggios, and ear training presented as separate concepts. First you memorize a bunch of scale dot patterns. Then you memorize a bunch of chords—some with fancy names—and you wonder how many of these you'll actually use. You may learn some music theory. You hear about tricks: take this scale and use the same notes, but move three steps this way, cross your fingers and play backwards and this mode becomes another mode, etc. But there doesn't seem to be any rhyme or reason, or if there is, you give up because it seems too complicated. Furthermore, each area—scales, chords, theory, and songs—remains separate. And a lot of it seems downright irrelevant. Faced with this, most guitarists eventually give up and reconcile themselves to the idea that they just "aren't strong on theory." Of those that continue to wade through a sea of details, many recognize that there is a deeper understanding that yet eludes them.

The missing secret is the knowledge that all these different things are really just different aspects of the *same thing*. This fundamental thing is the structure of music, seen through the guitar, and this is what *Fretboard Mastery* is really about. Attaining full competence with this information moves you beyond simply being a guitarist and into the realm of "pure" musician, since your knowledge of musical structure actually extends to any instrument. Here, we build up the entire picture the right way from ground level. Then everything falls into place as part of the interconnected whole.

That sounds good of course. But if you are like me, you may be wondering what this really means in practical terms. Here are some of the benefits you will gain:

- *Learning music becomes easier.* As you hear music, you can instantly envision the correct fret board shapes and patterns in your mind's eye. You just pick up your guitar and play it right the first time.

- *Creating music becomes easier.* You won't need to hunt for notes you hear in your imagination, either. As a result, songwriting becomes easier and faster. Instead of noodling through tired old patterns hoping to stumble across a new idea, you simply listen to your imagination and create from there. You are no longer tethered to the guitar—you can "write" music while you drive, take a shower, serve burgers, entertain the in-laws, etc.

- *Your musical ideas become more defined.* The musical ideas that you "hear" in your imagination become more clearly defined. Instead of vague impressions, they begin to arise more and more with specific pitch and rhythm.

- *You draw from a broader scope.* Any melody in any style of music is immediately perceived in its absolute terms. When melodies are so easy to assimilate, anything you hear—any song or commercial, any movie soundtrack, any musical idea in any style—can be applied to another context instantly. You can pull inspiration from anywhere.

- *You can evoke different moods freely.* You know how to create any mood in an instant by knowing which tones create each feeling. You can also play in any musical context without feeling lost.

- *No more bad notes while improvising.* When the fretboard/mind connection is strong, you don't play "wrong sounding" notes. You are playing from your inner ear, and you don't imagine sour notes, unless that's the quality you intentionally want to create! That doesn't mean you stick only to only "safe" scale tones, though. You are free to draw upon whatever tonality clashes or melodic tension you like. You are also no longer tied to a pre-learned bag of licks.

- *No more "blank spots" on the fretboard.* Of course some areas on the neck will always be more familiar than others, but with thorough use of the final portions of this book you will be free to move out of the familiar areas at the flip of a switch, whenever you feel the spontaneous urge to do so. The entire fretboard becomes your playground.

- *You gain a deeper understanding of the structure of music.* You can impress friends and enemies alike with your vast and intuitive knowledge of musical structure! What could be better than that?

These skills really add up to giving you more artistic control and therefore, more personal satisfaction as a musician. That's the ultimate benefit of *Fretboard Mastery.*

What Style Is This?

Most of the principles and skills taught here transcend style. Indeed, that is exactly what I am seeking to show you—how the same ideas play out across the board. Therefore, I've made an effort to touch on a range of styles including rock, alternative, metal, pop, classical, jazz, blues, etc. You will see how music works generally and how to point it in different stylistic directions.

However, I am a rock player and a shredder at heart, so that's where this book really stretches out in the end. Yet at the same time I believe simplicity often plays a more valuable role than complexity. Music is about expressing and creating emotion. So faster is not always better; it is just faster. And isn't a statement made stronger and bolder when non-essential portions are stripped away? In fact, writing good music is as much a process of knowing what to leave out as what to put in. So just because you *can* play a million miles an hour, doesn't mean you must do it constantly. It gets boring (to me at least). At this point my soloing style has become an outgrowth of melody. Sure I still play fast passages, but it is not really lick-based playing. It is just music, faster or slower, composed or improvised; it is imagination directly converted to the guitar. Here you will see how melody and soloing are actually two ends of the same thread, and all the principles that apply to melody also apply to soloing.

Regardless of my stylistic preferences, though, this book is not designed make your style a clone of mine. This book doesn't dictate a style. It shows you the underlying principles so you have the tools to quickly absorb *anything.* Indeed, you are encouraged to analyze those specific musical situations that interest you most—then they become a part of you and your style.

How to Use This Book

In a word: *patience*. This isn't a book to whip through and quickly leave behind. Hit a portion of it for a while, then set it aside and take a breather. Let it soak in. Look for the concepts you've learned here within the other music you play and learn. Then come back to this book and tackle another portion, or review a section to anchor it better in your experience. Like *Speed Mechanics*, this is a book you can use for years to come, constantly improving your musical abilities and understanding of the guitar.

Also, realize that this is not easy stuff. Let me repeat that: *This is not easy stuff!* Some of the skills presented here may take months or years to really nail down fully. So don't sweat it if your progress is slow. This is a rather difficult subject. On top of that, it raises the bar. Very few players attain anything near full proficiency with this. You don't have to achieve full proficiency to be a great player, to write good songs, or to become successful in the music business. Yes, the skills presented here can help you in those pursuits, but they aren't a requirement. Think of the material in this book as "extra credit." It is only necessary for those of you who have a personal desire to take your abilities to the highest artistic levels. So give yourself credit for even attempting this book, and regard every gain here as added value!

Yet, the challenge I present to you in these pages is certainly not impenetrable. The inspiration you feel as you progress, combined with the practical benefits of your new skills, will propel you forward. Just expect it to be a "slow burn." Stick with the program and you *will* gradually absorb it, without a doubt.

So here is how should you approach this book: Devote a little time to it each day, realizing you are gaining ground, little by little. Work this into your other practice activities, including whatever books, methods, technique exercises, songs, and solos interest you. Don't judge your progress by how many pages you have completed, or by those yet remaining. Judge only by positive results—specifically your increasing awareness in hearing, perceiving, and understanding.

Each person begins at a somewhat different level for each of the various skill-sets presented here. One section may be easy for you, while another may seem baffling beyond belief. That's okay. It just means you need extra time in that area. Come back and review it as needed. Remember, it is the skill development we are after here—not simply getting through any particular exercise. So if you finish a section but feel you haven't really got a good handle on it, hit it again or make up your own similar exercises. Whatever it takes, keep hammering away.

Finally, I should mention that there are some fairly challenging playing examples in the book, but honing your physical technique is not the point of *Fretboard Mastery*. These are simply here because they illustrated the concept at hand. For this reason, I have not played them fast and slow, but simply at full tempo. If you feel under-equipped to deal with anything from a technique standpoint, I encourage you to apply the concepts from *Speed Mechanics for Lead Guitar* and develop your chops as necessary.

The Musical Staff

You don't have to be a proficient sight-reader to use this book, since the musical staff is largely tangential to my approach to the fretboard. The staff is simply a means of communicating musical ideas. It is not the only means to do so. Music, after all, is *sound* and not the written notation on a page.

However, the staff is a handy way to show some types of musical ideas very clearly. So when it is necessary or helpful I will use the staff, particularly in Part III. As a starting point for this method, you should be familiar with the pitches on the musical staff and their corresponding notes on the guitar, at least in open position. If this is totally new to you, pick up a sight-reading book for guitar, or a basic "book 1" guitar method to learn at least the basics of reading staff notation before going deep into this book.

INTRODUCTION

Musicians learn to manipulate sound in order to create emotion in the listener. To do this effectively, it helps to have good "handles"—or ways of thinking about the sounds we are using—so we can "grab them" intellectually and make them do our bidding. We create these "handles" by naming and categorizing the different aspects of sound. That's called *music theory*. But of course you don't have to know the proper naming conventions to play good stuff. Always remember that it's the music itself that is the real thing, and the names we use to parse different aspects of it are merely labels of convenience. Music is the master, and theory is the servant. Music is real, and theory is...well, just a theory...a way of thinking about things. It's not the only way to think about things. It's just one particularly useful way.

Nevertheless, there is tremendous value in developing the mental structure of music theory. We can see further, build more elaborate ideas, and even cross-pollinate concepts to create entirely new concepts. Had we not engaged in this labeling effort, we would not even be aware of the existence of most of these ideas, let alone be able to manipulate them in novel ways. So there is value in music theory.

Music theory is the systematic parsing of the elements of music. It's good to learn, but sometimes we have to remind ourselves to stop parsing and simply listen! Don't lose sight of the fact that music, and the emotion it conveys, is the point of it all. Theory exists to serve the creation of music.

Let There Be Sound

At a fundamental level, music is simply an arrangement of sounds in time. And here we have the first hatchet-stroke of theory, as it cleaves apart a "sound" component from a "time" component. We call the time aspect *rhythm*, and on a piece of written music, the time (or rhythm) stretches out horizontally. It moves from left to right as time passes

Time moves from left to right (horizontal)

The sound component can be further divided into two subcomponents: *timbre* and *pitch*. Timbre refers to the quality of sound, or tone of an instrument. For example, you can easily tell the difference between a guitar and a piano because they have a different *timbre*. The word "tone" is also used generally to describe something similar—a distorted guitar tone versus a clean guitar tone, for example. Or a muddy, bassy tone versus a thin, trebly tone.

On the other hand, *pitch* refers to a specific level of "highness" or "lowness." Pitch can be measured in Hertz, which is the number of vibrations per second of a frequency. Functionally, however, pitch is usually labeled with the letter names we have come to call *notes* (e.g., A, B, C♯, D♭). Pitch is mapped vertically on the musical staff, with higher-sounding pitches corresponding to higher placement and lower-sounding pitches corresponding to lower placement.

Pitch is indicated up and down (vertical)

People new to music, or with an otherwise undeveloped ear, sometimes get *tone* and *pitch* confused. They are, however, totally separate issues. Just plug in your electric guitar to demonstrate this: play the same note with the bass control up and treble down, then play the same note again with the bass control down and treble up. Different *tone,* same pitch.

Of the three main features of music (*rhythm, timbre/tone,* and *pitch*), the average listener probably notices the first two qualities more, at least initially. Pitch comes into play to a degree along with rhythm and tone, of course. But it is the "sleeper" aspect in a sense. Its effect is less immediately obvious. In the long run, however, it is pitch that plays the biggest role in locking music into our long-term memory. What follows in this book relates to an analysis of the subtleties of pitch. Music theory is largely an analysis of interactions between sets of pitches.

Scales, modes, keys, chords, and all the like are the children of Western music theory. At a basic level, all of these concepts are simply describing various sets of letter-named pitches. To speak about these different sets of pitches in a useful way—to tell one apart from the next—we must have a way to compare them. We do this by measuring them. Then we affix a name upon every possible distance between pitches. We call these various distances between pitches *intervals.* Armed with this musical measuring stick, we can separate and evaluate the fluid world of music.

Building on Solid Ground

The working structure of music begins with *intervals.* They are the building blocks of all the larger musical structures. Every musical structure—that is, every conceivable set of pitches—may be defined by its intervals.

Interval: A specified distance between two pitches. Intervals define every possible relationship between pitches.

Let's consider a few intervals. Two pitches that are the same are said to be in *unison.* That's an interval of "0," or no distance at all. When you tune one string to another on the guitar by the standard relative tuning method, you are employing unison intervals. Next comes the distance of one fret—for example, from the first fret on any string up to the second fret on that same string. This is an interval called a *half step.* The distance of two frets—from the first fret on a string up to the third fret on that string—is an interval called a *whole step.*

There are many more interval names. But first, consider these facts:

- Every interval has its own unique name.
- Every interval has its own unique sound.
- Every interval has its own unique shape on the fretboard.

So we can learn each interval by its name, sound, and shape. As we do this in Part I, keep in mind that you are not learning three different things—you are learning three different aspects of *one thing.* This is the foundation for everything else that follows.

After learning the intervals, you will see how they combine to make various larger musical structures and you will learn to recognize all of these by ear. In Part II we expand that knowledge over the full primary shapes. Then all these structures are woven together into a coherent musical fabric in Part III. Parts IV and V complete the fretboard by expanding what you already know into the other areas of the neck and adding a few more advanced concepts. At the end, we take a look at a full song to apply everything you have learned and test your ear.

Tuning Notes

It's time to tune up. Track 1 on the accompanying audio CD is the low E string in standard tuning. Tune relative to this or use your electronic tuner.

Standard Tuning: Low E string reference pitch

Track 1

Notes on the Fretboard

The letter names of the notes on the fretboard in standard tuning are a starting point for this method. If you don't know them well, take some time and memorize them now.

First, take those on the lowest two strings—the E and A strings, or strings 6 and 5, respectively. Play up and down the natural notes below saying the names out loud until you have fully memorized their positions and can locate any one of them without pause.

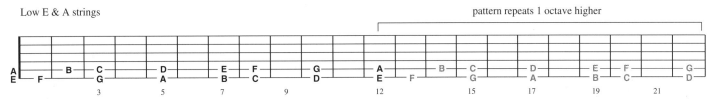

> FYI: The frets in between the natural notes labeled above actually each have two possible names—either the flat of the next higher note or the sharp of the next lower one. So for example, the fourth fret on string 5 is called either C♯ or D♭. These are called *enharmonic* equivalents. The correct spelling depends on the musical context.

Next, look at the middle set of strings—the D and G strings, or strings 4 and 3. The pattern of notes here is exactly the same as on the lower strings, except two frets higher. If you are more familiar with the note names on the lower strings (as most guitarists are due to their barre-chord-playing experience), you can use the octave shape shown below to transfer note names up to these middle strings. However, this "shortcut" is only a temporary assist. You should memorize the names well enough that you simply *know* them directly, as they appear on strings 3 and 4, without having to make any "octave transfers."

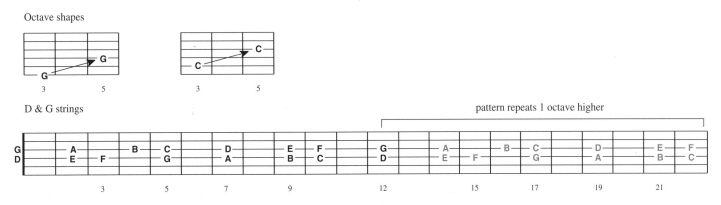

Finally we arrive at the upper strings—the B and E strings, or strings 2 and 1. There is no easy way to deal with the B string. Just memorize it. The last one, however, is a piece of cake. The high E string has the same notes as the low E string (just two octaves higher).

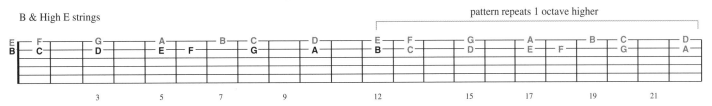

PART I: A Foundation for Music

Your musical foundation begins with intervals. These will eventually become as familiar to you as good, trusted friends—here to serve you for a lifetime of music. (And that's more than you can say about a lot of friends!) We will start with simple intervals and build them into scales, triads, and finally, melody.

Simple Intervals

Simple intervals are those contained within one octave. There are twelve half steps per octave in Western music, so there are a total of thirteen conceivable simple intervals (twelve plus unison). We'll first consider just eight of them. Below, these lucky eight are shown relative to the starting pitch of A. Play each, memorizing their names and shapes on the guitar.

 Example 1 – **Interval Names, Shapes & Sounds**

Track 2

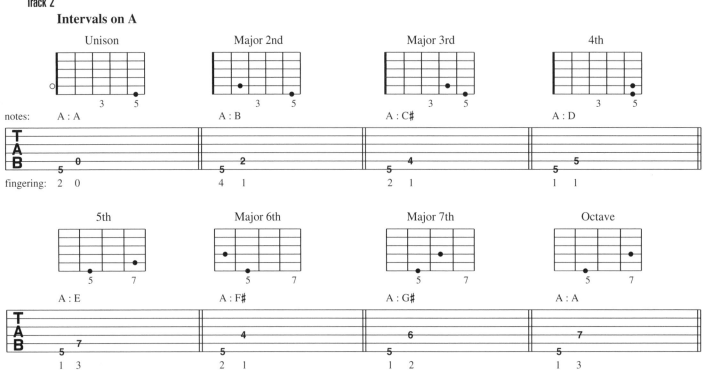

Play each interval shape below on the guitar and write in its correct name. (Answers on page 161.)

 Example 2 – **Interval Shape ➞ Name**

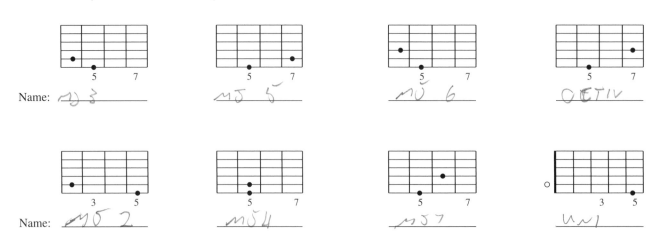

Next, given only the names, locate each interval on the guitar and play the correct shapes. You should be able to find each immediately, without hesitation. If you need more practice, just write out a long series of these interval names at random and play through the shapes as fast as possible.

Example 3 - **Interval Name → Shape**

a)	5th	i)	4th
b)	4th	j)	Major 2nd
c)	Octave	k)	Unison
d)	Unison	l)	5th
e)	Major 6th	m)	Major 3rd
f)	Major 7th	n)	Major 7th
g)	Octave	o)	Octave
h)	Major 3rd	p)	Major 6th

If we put all these tones together and play them in order, we have the *major scale*. In Example 4, notice the location of the major scale's numbered tones. These correspond to the intervals found between each note and the root of the scale (in this case, A). Notice all the interval shapes are hiding inside this scale.

Example 4 - **The A Major Scale**

Track 3

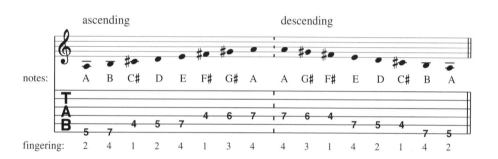

Next we are going to listen to some intervals and identify them purely by their sound alone. But first, here is a little trick you can use if you run into trouble:

Track 4

TIP: If you aren't certain what interval you are hearing, sing up or down the major scale from the root note and count the tones. When you reach the correct note, which is the same pitch as you heard in the interval in question, you will know which scale step it is, and therefore, what interval you are hearing. Listen to CD track 4 for an example of how this works. Keep in mind, however, that eventually you want to memorize the sound of each interval to the point that you can recognize it immediately without having to sing any "in between" scale tones.

For the next example, listen to each interval played on CD track 5 and identify it by its sound. Then play the interval shape you think it is. Does it sound the same? If not, back up and try again. When you get a match, write the interval name in the spaces on the following page. (Answers on page 161.) All these intervals will begin on the same pitch of A.

TIP: Use the pause button on your CD. After hearing an example, pause the disc immediately to hold those pitches in your mind until you can identify them.

Example 5 - **Interval Sound → Name, Shape**

a) _____   g) _____   m) _____

b) _____   h) _____   n) _____

c) _____   i) _____   o) _____

d) _____   j) _____   p) _____

e) _____   k) _____   q) _____

f) _____   l) _____

TIP: You may need more practice with this. Write down a long random list of these interval names and have a friend play them for you. Identify each by ear. Alternatively you could record a long list of intervals and simply play them back. Continue doing this until you can name them all by sound alone.

Now go over all the preceding examples, and this time *sing* the pitches of each interval as you play them. If you can't sing, just *hum* the best you can. If you can't hum, *try*. It really doesn't matter how good or bad you sound. It just matters that you do it! If the notes are too low for your voice, feel free to sing everything up an octave higher.

Repeat examples 1, 4, and 5, singing/humming each pitch as you play it.

FYI: Why singing? Well, we may just make a vocalist out of you yet, but that's not the reason for it. Your inner ear is intimately connected with your voice. When you sing a note, you hold a very clear perception of it in your mind. So singing what you play anchors these intervals into your mind much better and helps you learn them faster.

Now it's time to take it up a notch. Below you are given a set of interval names. First play and sing the starting pitch (we are using A), then visualize the location of the higher note on the fretboard for the second note of that interval. But *before* you pick that second note, sing or hum its pitch first. Then play it on the guitar to confirm the accuracy of your vocalization. CD track 6 demonstrates.

Example 6 - **"Vocal-leading" Interval Exercises**

a) 5th   i) Major 7th
b) Major 3rd   j) Major 6th
c) 4th   k) 5th
d) Major 2nd   l) Major 3rd
e) Major 3rd   m) 4th
f) 5th   n) Major 3rd
g) Major 6th   o) Major 2nd
h) Octave   p) Unison

TIP: Use the same scale trick as before if necessary. That is, sing up or down the major scale, counting the tones to arrive at the correct note. Gradually you will become familiar with certain standout intervals, like a 5th for example, and you can use these as "starting points" instead of always starting with the root. Of course the goal is to go directly to each interval without using any intervening tones.

Relativity

The phrase "everything is relative" is certainly true in music. An interval of a 5th always sounds pretty much the same, regardless of its absolute pitch. The specific starting point only determines its relative level of "highness" or "lowness." Each interval also maintains its same fretboard shape up and down the neck, so all you have to do is slide the whole thing up or down to go higher or lower. Pretty easy! Example 7 shows some intervals moved to a different starting point.

Example 7 - **Moving Interval Shapes**

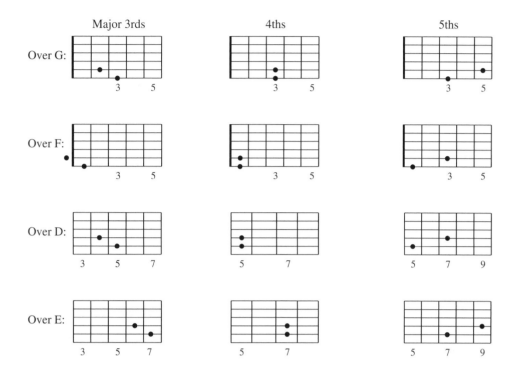

FYI: This is the beauty of the guitar—it accurately conveys the relative nature of pitch. But this beauty comes at a price, which we'll see in a moment.

Listen to each of the following intervals on the CD track 7, identify the names by sound, and write them in the spaces below. This time the lower starting pitch will change. (Answers on page 161.) Don't worry about the exact pitches; it is just the interval names that we are after here.

Track 7

Example 8 - **Ear Training with Intervals**

a) _____   f) _____

b) _____   g) _____

c) _____   h) _____

d) _____   i) _____

e) _____   j) _____

The guitar certainly allows for easy relative pitch changes, but this convenience has a price; it gives us multiple places to play the exact same pitch. This means that intervals don't have just one shape, but several. (Nooooo!!!) This is where things can get a little hairy. But stick with the plan and we'll get through them. Memorize the following alternate shapes now.

Example 9 - **Alternate Interval Shapes**

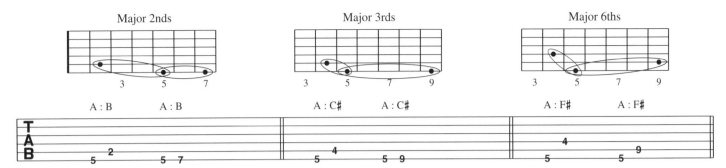

Presentation

Sometimes *how* you say something is just as important as *what* you say. Intervals can be like that too. Their presentation can drastically affect how they are perceived. There are two ways they may be presented: *melodically* and *harmonically*. When the notes follow one another, as in a melody, we say it is a *melodic interval*. When the notes sound simultaneously, as in a chord, we say it is a *harmonic interval*.

Up to this point, we have been playing intervals as a little of both. The notes were played one after another (as a melodic interval), yet they were allowed to also ring together (as a harmonic interval). A true melodic interval consists of a pure leap from one note to the next without the pitches sounding together.

Presented harmonically, intervals evoke very different qualities. Now there are actually three different elements to hear—the two separate pitches plus the texture of their interaction. Some intervals blend nicely together, and we say they are *consonant*. Others seem to clash severely, and we call them *dissonant*. Strike the notes of the harmonic intervals below simultaneously and listen carefully to their sonic texture.

Example 10 – **Melodic vs. Harmonic Intervals**

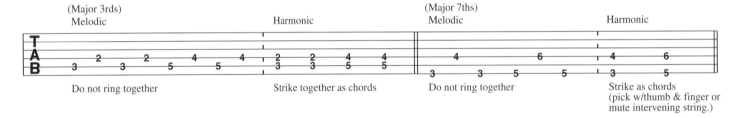

The unison and octave are pure consonances. The 5th is also a powerful consonance. The 4th is considered a consonance, unless played in the low register. The major 3rd is a consonance with a richer interaction that sounds colorful and somewhat at rest. The major sixth sounds colorful and bright, but less restful than the 3rd. The 7th and 2nd intervals are *dissonant*, with audible "beats" between them.

Example 11 – **Consonance vs. Dissonance**

...And Justice for All?

Some intervals come in just one flavor, and they are called *perfect* intervals. Others have split personalities, and can appear in either of two flavors. These are called *imperfect* intervals. This naming scheme is certainly one of the great injustices of music theory as it suggests some kind of hierarchy—as if one set is better than the other. Maybe we'd be better off with *fixed* and *changeable*, although I'd have preferred *righteous* and *schizoid*. Nevertheless, we seem to be stuck with it.

Additionally, the two versions of imperfect intervals are known as *major* and *minor*—another rather uninspired naming. (Perhaps *strong/weak*, *positive/negative*, *yin/yang*, or *masculine/feminine* would have been more descriptive?)

Perfect	Imperfect
"We have no flaws! We are righteous and destined to rule over all lesser intervals! Beware of our strength."	"We are the wretched, inferior intervals, doomed to roam evermore in a ceaseless duality of light and dark!"
unison	major/minor 2nd
4th	major/minor 3rd
5th	major/minor 6th
octave	major/minor 7th

The perfect intervals are below on the left. Taken together, notice their angular-looking, "square-ish" shape. Group these in your mind. Then look at the major imperfect interval shapes on the right. This pattern looks somewhat more interesting, with various angles to the starting note—maybe even colorful?

Example 12 - **Perfect Intervals vs. Major Intervals**

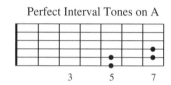
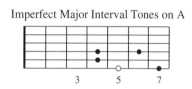

FYI: Combine the tones above and you have the full pattern of the major scale.

Next, let's consider the minor intervals. All the minors are found a half step below their major counterparts, at the bottom of this cruel heap of lies. Because a *flat* sign (♭) means to lower a pitch one half step, they may be interchangeably called "minor 2nd" or "♭2nd," "minor 3rd" or "♭3rd," "minor 6th" or "♭6th," and "minor 7th" or "♭7th." Below are their fretboard shapes, along with their common alternate shapes.

Track 8

Example 13 - **Minor Intervals**

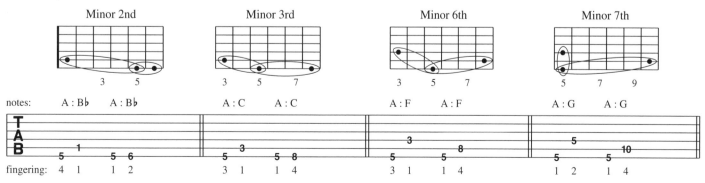

If the four perfect intervals plus the four major intervals created the major scale, it would stand to reason that the four perfect intervals plus the four minor intervals would give us the minor scale. That *would* make sense. But it would also be wrong. Just like any language, music has its exceptions. The natural minor scale is actually formed with a minor 3rd, minor 6th, minor 7th, and a *major* 2nd. Natural minor is typically seen as the musical opposite of major. It sounds basically dark and sad, or gothic.

Track 9

Example 14 – **The A Natural Minor Scale**

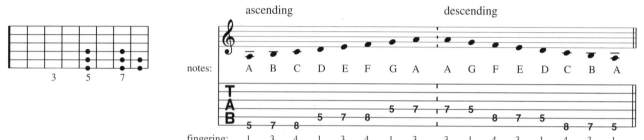

Now try some ear training with the minor intervals. Listen to each one on CD track 10, pause the disc, and identify the interval by sound only. Then write in the interval name below. (Answers on page 161.)

TIP: You can use the natural minor scale to help identify these minor intervals, just as we had used the major scale earlier. The minor 2nd is not in the natural minor scale, but it's a small adjustment to make—you simply drop the 2nd step of the scale a half step to find minor 2nd.

Track 10

Example 15 - **Ear Training for Minor Intervals**

a) _____

b) _____

c) _____

d) _____

e) _____

f) _____

g) _____

h) _____

i) _____

Major and Minor Scales

So what exactly is a scale anyway? A *scale* is simply a group of pitches that have some practical use in music. Basically, if we look at a bit of music and pull out all the pitches it uses, then stack them up and play in order up or down, we have a scale.

The major scale is said to lie at the foundation of Western music generally speaking, but specific styles may rely more on other scales. Still, the major scale is very important and is the starting point for any serious scale study. As it has seven different notes per octave, it is known as a *diatonic* (seventone) scale. It sounds basically bright, happy, or triumphant, and very naturally "melodic" to our ears. The natural minor scale is another diatonic scale that sounds dark and sad—the opposite of major. It can be considered the second most important scale in Western music.

What makes a scale sound the way it does? It's not the specific pitches it contains; it is the relationship of these pitches to one another—just as we saw with intervals. In fact, you can view a scale as being made up of the sum of the intervals contained within it.

Scale: A particular arrangement of pitches that has some practical use in music. The relationship of the pitches to one another gives a scale its characteristic quality. Or to say it another way, the sound of a scale can be seen to arise from the sum of its intervallic components.

Alternatively, we can also describe a specific scale structure by looking at the melodic intervals that lie between the steps of the scale. Viewed from one to the next, consecutively, these create a specific pattern of whole (W) and half (H) steps. This pattern is sometimes called a *scale formula*.

Example 16 shows the major and minor scale both in the standard positional pattern as well as stretched out on a single string. (Notice the two ways that whole steps can appear, depending on whether the notes lay on the same or adjacent strings.) The major scale formula is two segments of W-W-H separated by a W step. The natural minor scale starts with two W-H segments separated by a W step, then W-W. step,

Example 16 - **Scale Formulas**

Track 11

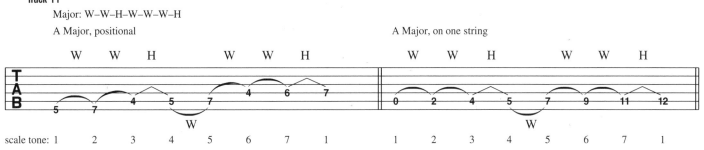

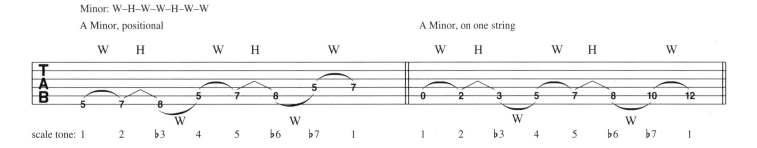

Memorize these structures and their scale tones!

FYI: Another name for a *whole step* is a major 2nd, and another name for a *half step* is a minor 2nd. We tend to use the whole-step and half-step names in situations where the focus is on the intervals as pure distance. The major and minor 2nd names, on the other hand, tend to suggest a tonal center, or root. But these "rules" are not ironclad, and you may see the terms used interchangeably.

Play the scales below, *singing* along with each as you play it. Just as we saw with intervals, when we move these larger scale structures up and down the neck they retain the same overall quality. They simply sound a little higher or lower.

Track 12

Example 17 - **Ear Training with Scales**

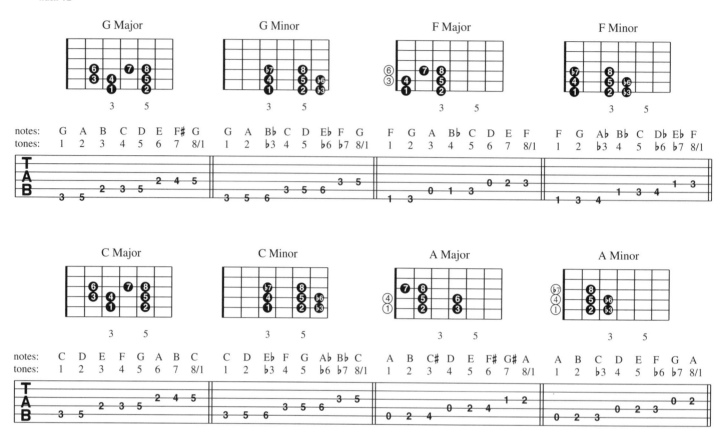

FYI: There is no doubt that scales have powerful emotional attachments for us. But why do we universally tend to associate similar subjective qualities to a particular arrangement of tones? That's a good question. The answer lies perhaps with the *overtone series*. Overtones are kind of "silent" notes that are part of the fundamental note we play or sing. It's beyond the scope of this book to explain the concept fully, but we can explain the basis.

When we play a C note on most instruments, we're not actually hearing just a C note. There are several harmonic overtones that are happening above (or "over") the fundamental note. The first one is an octave higher, the second is an octave-and-a-5th, the third is two octaves, the fourth is two octaves-and-a-major 3rd, and they continue on upward, getting closer and closer together. In fact, you can see this overtone series in action by playing harmonics along an open string on the guitar. Play harmonics on the A string, for example, at frets 12, 7, 5, 4, and on and on closer to the nut, and you'll get the picture. We're technically "hearing" all of those notes when we play that open string, even though we aren't aware of it.

The lower overtones, which are the most prominent, suggest a major tonality (with the major 3rd being a fairly strong overtone). This is perhaps why major 3rds sound brighter or more consonant to us and minor 3rds sound darker or more dissonant. The minor 3rd is "going against the grain," so to speak, of the natural overtone series.

The Root of All Evil

No, it's not the love of money. It's the *tritone*—the interval found between the 4th and 5th. This most turbulent dissonance has spawned a musical wave of destruction second to none. Where would metal be without the tritone?

The tritone also goes by the names *diminished 5th* or *augmented 4th*. This is because diminished means lowered (*flatted*) one fret, and augmented means raised (*sharped*) one fret. But wait... Didn't *minor* mean lowered one fret? And the perfect intervals couldn't be altered, right? Well, that's what they would have you believe. But in fact, *any* interval can be diminished or augmented, and this is in addition to the major/minor designation. So you could in theory have a diminished minor 3rd, for example, which would be the same pitch as a major 2nd. Things get complicated fast, as each interval suddenly has a huge variety of possible names. But this is a labeling issue arising from the notational staff system, which is built upon the structure of the keyboard layout, blah, blah, blah. Players of chromatic instruments (like the guitar) don't need to get hung up on this. Just blame the piano and its ridiculous insistence upon idolizing the diatonic structure by engraving it into its black/white key pattern. Let's move on.

Here is the tritone on A. Listen for its extreme dissonance, which is further intensified by a distorted tone. When heard as a melodic leap, the tritone conveys an odd sort of "twisting" to the ear.

Track 13

Example 18 - **The Tritone**

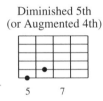

Diminished 5th
(or Augmented 4th)

5   7

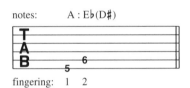

notes: A : Eb(D#)

fingering: 1   2

FYI: In the middle ages, when European music was primarily centered on the church, the tritone was literally called "the devil in music" (*diabolus in musica*). They went to great lengths to avoid it, establishing a system of chromatic alteration called "falsified music" (*musica ficta*). At first, the system wasn't written down, as it was considered so obvious as to not need explanation. The first accidental signs (sharps and flats in the staff) were in fact referred to as *signum asinorum*, as apparently only an ass would have to be told! But eventually, music grew more complex and accidental signs became necessary. Today, our modern ears have developed such a tolerance for conflict and dissonance that the tritone sounds at best only slightly unusual.

Triads and Arpeggios

A triad is a three-note chord. Below are the chord formulas for the four different types of triads:

Major:	1-3-5
Minor:	1-b3-5
Diminished:	1-b3-b5
Augmented:	1-3-#5

Of course a chord means that the notes are played simultaneously and ring together (harmonically). On the other hand, an *arpeggio* is what you have if you play the notes of a chord played in succession (melodically). Here, we are going to play the chord triads as arpeggios because it is rather difficult to sing three notes simultaneously. Play each arpeggio and sing along.

Track 14 Example 19 – **Arpeggiated Triads**

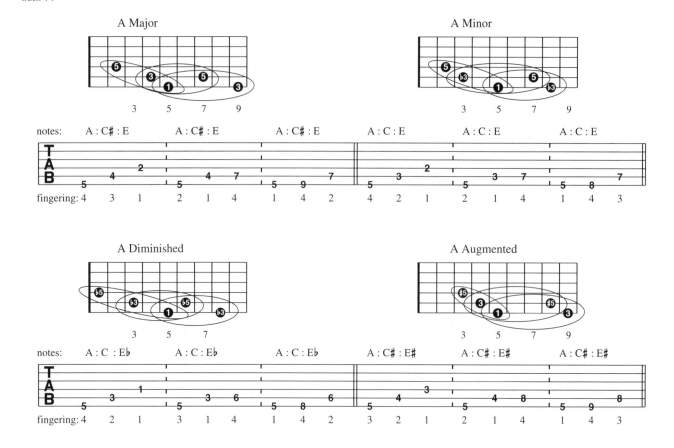

Now listen to CD track 15 and determine what type of triad each one is by its sound alone. Then write it in the space provided. (Answers on page 161.)

Track 15 Example 20 - **Ear Training with Triads**

a) _____   h) _____   n) _____

b) _____   i) _____   o) _____

c) _____   j) _____   p) _____

d) _____   k) _____   q) _____

e) _____   l) _____   r) _____

f) _____   m) _____   s) _____

g) _____

Melodic Tendency

On a functional level, when tones of a melody sit against a backing chord they fall into one of two general categories. They are either *chord tones* or *non-chord tones*. All chord tones share the quality of sitting comfortably against the backing chord, while the non-chord tones are somewhat unsettled and can be thought of as wanting to move. First, let's practice identifying chord tones. Then we'll take a look at the non-chord tones.

In example 21, a chord is sounded in the left stereo channel, and four chord tones are played in sequence in the right channel. Identify the scale tones in the right channel relative to the chord and write them down in the blank space provided. (Answers on page 161.) The backing chords are all 5th type power chords (no 3rd), so that either type of 3rd can appear on the right.

TIP: Chord tones are roots, 3rds, and 5ths. The 3rd, whether major or minor, is called the *color tone* since it "colors" a chord either major or minor. In this example, label major 3rds as "3" and minor 3rds as "♭3." The octave is also a root and can be labeled as "1." However, in this case we will use "8" to differentiate it from the lower root.

Track 16

Example 21 - **Ear Training for Chord Tones**

a) _____   h) _____

b) _____   i) _____

c) _____   j) _____

d) _____   k) _____

e) _____   l) _____

f) _____   m) _____

g) _____   n) _____

The non-chord tones are 2nds, 4ths, and 6ths. These sound somewhat unsettled against the backing chord and can be seen to want to move toward a stable pitch (chord tone) where they can come to rest. Sustaining a non-chord tone against this natural inclination creates a distinct tension, which we call a *suspension*. The 7ths also create a strong pull, but of a somewhat different nature. For our purposes here we will classify them as non-chord tones, too, for now.

Let's look at these unsettled tones in greater detail. Not only do they want to move, they want to move to very specific places—generally the closest stable tone. So a 2nd will want to either fall to the root or rise to the 3rd. The 4th wants to fall to the 3rd or rise to the 5th. A 6th wants to fall to a 5th, and the 7th wants to rise to the octave root.

FYI: The motion of a pitch from a state of tension to a state of rest is called *resolution*. One rule of melodic resolution is that half steps pull harder than whole steps. In addition, gravitation to the roots are extra powerful. Even the least musically-trained among us may recognize the inevitability of a major 7th-to-octave pull, and the dramatic minor 2nd-to-root pull.

Each of the resolutions below are played against an A root note on CD track 17. Listen for the characteristic suspension and subsequent resolution of each one, then play it on your guitar. No rush here. Let it hang, and savor the vibe. Meditate on it for a time, listening deeply, and let its quality and sonic texture really "sink in." Eventually you will begin to "hear" the suspended tone telling you where it wants to go in your own inner ear.

Track 17

Example 22 - **Melodic Resolution**

a) 4th falling to major 3rd (1/2 step)
b) major 2nd rising to major 3rd (whole step)
c) major 6th falling to 5th (whole step)
d) 4th rising to 5th (whole step)
e) major 2nd falling to root (whole step)
f) major 7th rising to root (1/2 step)

g) major 2nd rising to minor 3rd (1/2 step)
h) minor 6th falling to 5th (1/2 step)
i) minor 7th rising to root (whole step)
j) minor 2nd falling to root (1/2 step)
k) augmented 4th rising to 5th (1/2 step)

FYI: When tones pull to resolve upward (rising), they are called *leading* tones. When they pull to resolve downward (falling), they are called *leaning* tones.

In example 23, first you will hear a chord in the left channel followed by some tones in the right channel. Pause the CD after you hear each one and run that brief melody through your mind to identify the scale steps relative to that chord. Write them below. (Answers on page 161.)

 Example 23 – **Ear Training: Chord and Non-Chord Tones**

Track 18

a) _____ h) _____

b) _____ i) _____

c) _____ j) _____

d) _____ k) _____

e) _____ l) _____

f) _____ m) _____

g) _____ n) _____

TIP: First latch on to any chord tones you hear. Then move forward or backward from those "landmarks" to fill in the blanks if necessary. You can also use the scale "trick" discussed earlier to identify any problem tones. Just hold the unknown pitch in your mind then sing up the scale, keeping the steps in mind, until you locate it.

Melodic Fragments

Now we are getting closer to real music. We're not quite there yet, but closer. Play the following short melodies on the guitar and sing along. Then, sing it *without* playing at all—simply *envision* the fretboard pattern and location of each note as you sing it. Each melody in example 24 uses the tonal center of G.

TIP: Sing the actual tonal (intervallic) number for each note instead of "ah, ah, ah..."

Example 24 – **Short Melodic Fragments**

Track 19

Did you notice that example 24g used the major 7th instead of the minor 7th? If so, good job! We'll find out what this is called later on.

FYI: Moving step-wise through a scale is known as *conjunct motion*. This means, for example, that if you were on the 4th tone of the scale, you only have two choices—moving up to the 5th or down to the 3rd. Skipping diatonic scale tones is known as *disjunct motion*. Look at example 24 again and write "C" for every instance of conjunct motion and "D" for every instance of disjunct motion. (Answers on page 161.)

Next, listen to the following melodies on CD track 20. Determine the tonal sequence of each phase by ear and write it in the space. To help you get started, listen for standout intervals you have learned to recognize best, or any strong resolutions you know. Then "fill in the blanks" as needed. Singing stepwise up or down the relevant portions of the major or minor scale can be particularly helpful if the melody happens to skip any scale tones. (Answer on page 161.)

Track 20

Example 25 – **Ear Training with Melody**

    a) Root=A _____

    b) Root=A _____

    c) Root=A _____

    d) Root=G _____

    e) Root=G _____

    f) Root=E _____

    g) Root=D _____

    h) Root=D _____

    i) Root=E _____

Now, get some blank staff/tab manuscript paper and transcribe, or write out, each of these short melodies. (You'll find some blank staff/tabs on page 164.) Then write in the intervallic tones under each note in the staff. The correct transcriptions appear in the appendix. Check your work against it to see how well you did.

TIP: Awareness of the numbered scale tones is generally more important than even knowing the letter-names of the notes you are using. This is because tonal numbers tell you something about how the pitches relate to one another, and therefore how they sound. The letter-named notes on the other hand only tell you a note's absolute pitch and nothing about its use or relationship to other notes.

At this point, you should have a good handle on the tones of the major and minor scales. You know how they look and sound on the four lower-sounding strings. You should be able to pick out melodic fragments and discern their musical structures by ear. If you have trouble with this, record your own melody exercises for more practice or have someone else play them for more ear training. Also, whenever you listen to the radio, pick out any vocal or instrumental melodies you hear—even bass lines— and try to identify their structures by ear, simultaneously imagining the corresponding fretboard shapes on the guitar. Then pick up your guitar when you can and test yourself to see how accurate you were.

Chromatic Melody

Now that we have covered the thirteen simple intervals, let's toss them all together and make a tonal "map." Below all the tones are shown covering every possible half step between the A roots. They are called *chromatic tones* because "chromatic" refers to notes that are a half step apart.

Example 26 – **Chromatic Tones Relative to A**

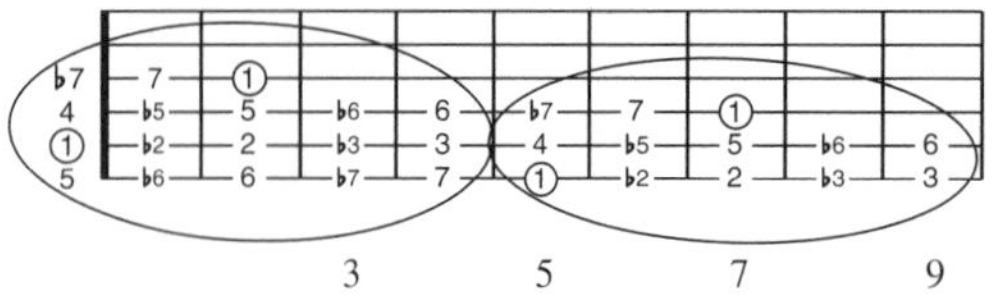

Listen to each melody in example 27 until you can hum along with it. Then identify the tonal structure by ear and write it down in the space. (Answers on page 161.) Finally, notice that the root note is also given for each melody. Since you have already identified the tonal structure AND you know where to find each note on the fretboard, you should be able to pick up your guitar and play that melody instantly. Make it sound the same as on the CD! Then write out each one on staff/tab and compare it to the transcriptions in the appendix.

Track 21

Example 27 - **Ear Training with Chromatics**

a) Root = A ______________________________

____

b) Root = G ______________________________

____

c) Root = E ______________________________

____

d) Root = E ______________________________

____

e) Root = A ______________________________

____

f) Root = A ______________________________

____

g) Root = F♯ ______________________________

____

FYI: When music mixes tones from different scales, new scales are created. We'll talk about exactly what these scales are in more detail later. For now, simply focus on identifying the correct location of each pitch and its intervallic tonal name (its number).

Scale/Voice Integration

When we play a regular pattern in a scale, which repeats sequentially higher or lower, we call it a scale *sequence*. Below, a common sequence pattern in threes is shown applied to the A major and A minor scale. Sing each note as you play up and down these scale sequences.

Track 22

Example 28 – **Scale Sequencing**

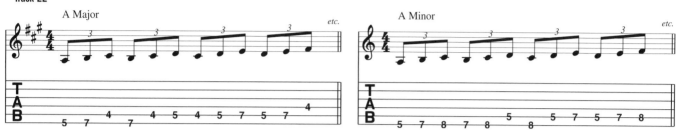

We could represent the ascending sequences above as 1-2-3, 2-3-4, 3-4-5, etc.; the descending sequence mirroring this would be 8-7-6, 7-6-5, etc. These numbers refer to the scale steps within the pattern and could apply to either a major or minor scale (or any other scale for that matter).

Below are a few more sequence patterns. Apply these to the major and minor scales in several different keys. Speed is not important here. What is crucial is that you *always sing accurately with every note as you play*. The purpose here is to better connect your inner ear to the fretboard.

1-2-3-4, 2-3-4-5, 3-4-5-6, etc.	8-7-6-5, 7-6-5-4, 6-5-4-3, etc.
1-2-3-4, 3-4-5-6, 5-6-7-8, etc.	8-7-6-5, 6-5-4-3, 4-3-2-1, etc.
1-2-3-1, 2-3-4-2, 3-4-5-3, etc.	8-7-6-8, 7-6-5-7, 6-5-4-6, etc.
1-3-1, 2-4-2, 3-5-3, etc.	8-6-8, 7-5-7, 6-4-6, etc.
1-3-5, 2-4-6, 3-5-7, etc.	8-6-4, 7-5-3, 6-4-2, etc.
1-3-2-3-4-3-2-1, 2-4-3-4-5-4-3-2, etc.	8-6-7-6-5-6-7-8, 7-5-6-5-4-5-6-7, etc.

Next we'll improvise contours and sequences within each scale, making it up "on the fly." Listen to the sample on CD track 23 to get the idea how this works. Start by playing evenly and using only conjunct motion (no skips). Speed is not particularly important here; take it as slow as necessary. The important thing here is to *sing every note as you play it*. As you get better at this you can speed up a little and begin to skip scale steps (disjunct motion) as you like.

Track 23

Example 29 - **Improvised Scale/Voice Exercises**

FYI: The term *contour* means an outline, shape, or curve in general usage. In music, a *scale contour* means that if we were to look at the notes written out on a musical staff and connect them with an imaginary line, you would see various shapes, or "contours" emerge. A sequence is a regularly repeating contour. So all sequences are contours, but not all contours are sequences. The example below shows this graphically.

Example 30 – **Scale Counters and Sequences**

PART II: Positional Scales and Chords

Here we will expand our interval and scale knowledge into multi-octave positional patterns. We'll also cover a variety of new scale types.

Crossing the Great Divide

In standard tuning, strings 3–6 are intervallically consistent. Each string is a perfect 4th (five half steps) apart. So the sound-shapes apply here without exception. But things change when we cross between strings 2 and 3, since the second string is tuned to only a major 3rd interval (four half steps) above the third string—one half step less than the others. Because of this, any fretboard shape that crosses an imaginary dividing line between strings 2 and 3 must be *raised one fret* to compensate for the lowered tuning and maintain the same musical structure. Things get back to normal between strings 1 and 2, as we are back to perfect 4th tuning there.

Caution: Don't proceed with these new shapes until you have all the normal interval shapes from Part I memorized well. It's best to learn the rules before you take on the exceptions.

Track 24

Example 31 – **Interval Shape Alterations**

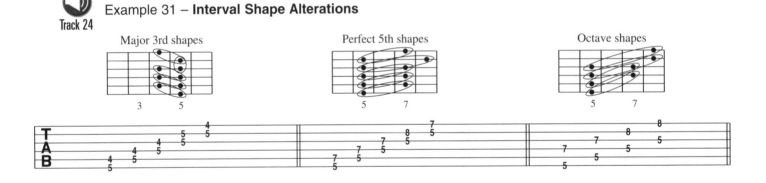

Regard each fretted note below as a root. Mark in the missing higher note for each named interval. (Answers on page 161.)

Example 32 – **Fill in the Missing Notes**

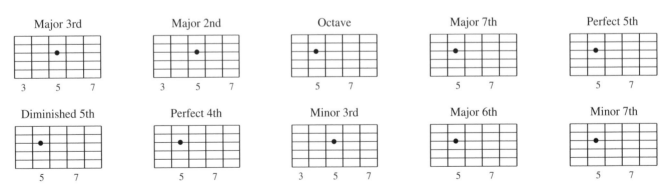

FYI: Shapes must be altered when we cross the dividing line between strings 2 and 3. This also commonly includes patterns on strings 1 and 3, and 2 and 4, since they also cross the dividing line.

Example 33 shows major scale and triad patterns as they are progressed upward string by string. Note how they shift up one fret when they hit string 2. Other than that, the patterns are identically shaped. So notice the shift, but at the same time look past it to see how the patterns are in a sense the same—at a "deeper" level of musical structure, after the tuning shift is accounted for.

Track 25

Example 33 – Scale and Triad Shape Alteration

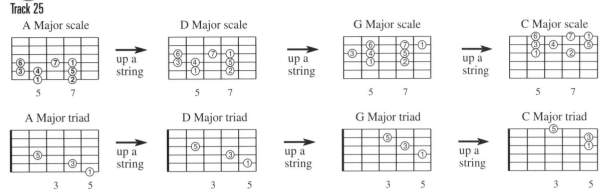

Two-Octave Major and Minor Scale Shapes

You already know the first octave shapes. The second octave begins on the top root note and repeats—but of course you must account for the second-string position shift.

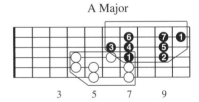

Example 34 – **Two-Octave A Major**

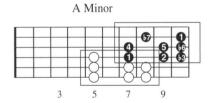

Example 35 – **Two-Octave A Minor**

Below, these two scales have been forced into a single physical position on the neck by moving some of the higher-octave notes up to the next higher string. These positional versions are the most common major and minor scale shapes.

Track 26

Example 36 – **Two-Octave Positional Scales**

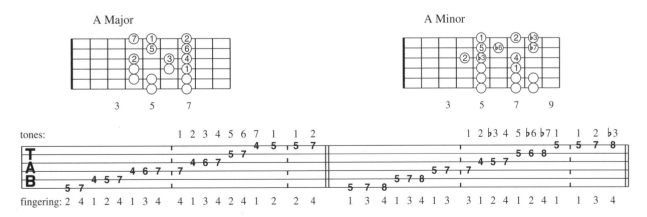

Below are the tones for the common major and minor barre chord and arpeggio shapes that correspond to the preceding positional scale patterns. Notice how each of the chord and arpeggio tones are totally encompassed within its corresponding scale. Think of the chord or arpeggio as a "skeleton" upon which the rest of the scale hangs and "fleshes out."

Example 37 – **Barre Chords and Arpeggios**

Track 27

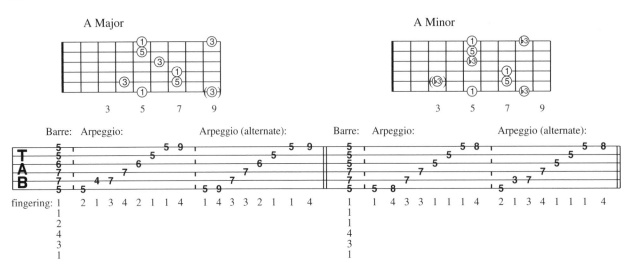

FYI: Major and minor chords are made up of roots, 3rds, and 5ths. Chords often contain more than three notes, however. This is achieved by adding octaves of chord tones. The specific order of chord tones that appear in a chord is called the *chord voicing*. There are many different possible voicings, with correspondingly different shapes, for any chord name.

Ideally, you want to see both the arpeggios and scale patterns together, superimposed on one another. This is the easiest way to gain insight into the function of each individual tone within a scale. If the tone is found in the arpeggio pattern, it is a chord tone. If not, it is a non-chord tone and creates a suspended feel if sustained over the root. Below, the chord tones are black, and the non-chord tones are grey.

Example 38 – **Superimposed Arpeggios and Scales**

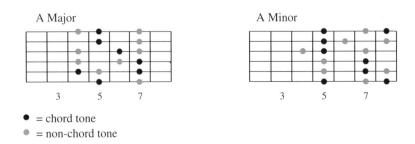

● = chord tone
● = non-chord tone

TIP: Scales are not dots! They are musical tones, each with its own distinct personality, function, and tendency. Don't just memorize the "dot" pattern; learn the position of every tone within that pattern. Then you really know the scale—i.e., you'll know how to use it melodically. Use the superimposed arpeggio shapes to help you define which tones are chord tones and which are non-chord tones. The arpeggios contain steps 1–3–5. The notes found in the scale but that are not in the arpeggio (the non-chord tones) are steps 2–4–6–7.

Test your knowledge by writing in all the tones in the diagram below. (Answers on page 161.)

Example 39 – **Upper Octave Scale Tones**

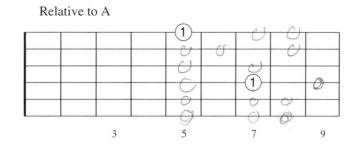

Relative to A

Since we are covering the higher-octave tones, let's also consider *compound intervals* briefly. Compound intervals are those greater than an octave. They can be seen as being made up of a simple interval plus an octave, and we usually call them by their simple interval names ("octave reduced") when the tones appear in scales or arpeggios. The compound names are used only when we refer to them specifically where the extra octave is relevant. In the figures below, the intervening octave is shown in gray to help you see the intervals within.

Example 40 – **Compound Intervals**

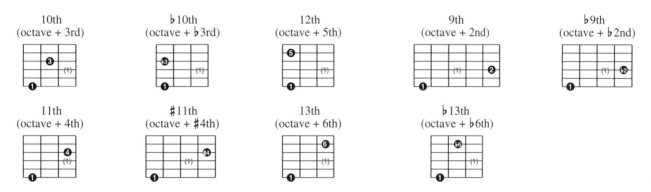

Now let's try some ear training in the upper octave range. All of the following melody fragments are based on the root note A. First, listen to each phrase and decipher its tonal structure by ear, then write it in the space below. (Answers on page 162.) Next, envision the note pattern on the fretboard that corresponds to that tonal structure and play that melody on your guitar. It should sound the same as on the CD. Finally, write it out. (Transcriptions are in the appendix to check your work.)

Track 28

Example 41 – **Ear Training in Upper Octave Range**

a) _____

b) _____

c) _____

d) _____

e) _____

f) _____

g) _____

h) _____

i) _____

j) _____

Seventh Chords

There are two types of seventh chords built upon the major triad. Take a major triad, toss an added minor 7th on top, and we have a *dominant 7th* chord (usually called simply a "7th chord"). Take a major triad and toss an added major 7th on top and we have a *major 7th* chord. There are also two types of sevenths built upon a minor triad. Take a minor triad, toss a minor 7th on top, and you have a *minor 7th* chord. Far less common is the *minor(major)7th* chord—a minor triad with an added major 7th tone.

Name:	Abbreviation:	Formula:
Dominant 7th	7	1–3–5–♭7
Minor 7th	m7	1–♭3–5–♭7
Major 7th	maj7	1–3–5–7
Minor (major 7th)	m(maj7)	1–♭3–5–7

Below are the arpeggio shapes for these 7th chord types with the root on string 6 and 5. Play up and down through each until you have them all memorized.

Example 42 – **7th Arpeggios**

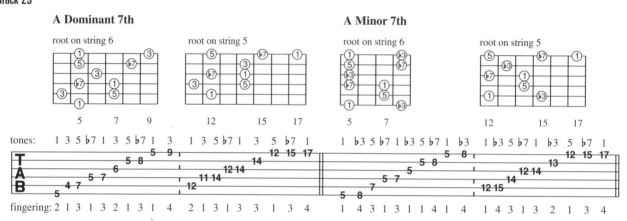

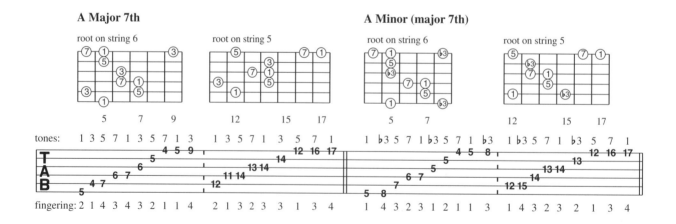

32

Now play each of the 7th chord shapes below and write in the chord type and the correct tones from low to high in the blank spaces. (Answers on page 162.)

Example 43 – **7th Chord Voicings**

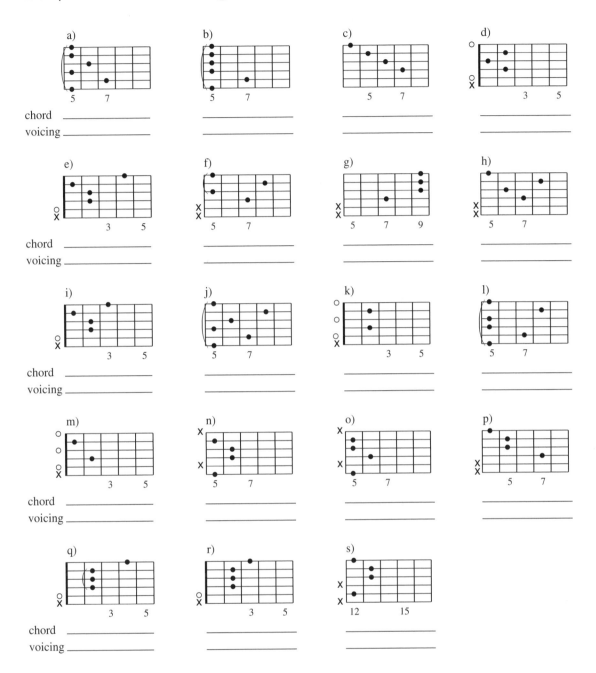

FYI: The major 7th and minor 7th arpeggios are subsets of the major and minor scale, respectively. That is to say, all the tones of the major 7th chord are found in the major scale, and all the tones of the minor 7th chord are found in the natural minor scale. On the other hand, the dominant 7th and minor (major 7th) arpeggios "cross-pollinate" between the two scales. That is, the dominant 7th uses a major scale for 1–3–5 but adds ♭7 from the minor scale. The minor (major 7th) uses the minor scale for 1–♭3–5 but adds 7 from the major scale.

Pentatonic and Blues Scales

Pentatonic literally means five-tone. So beginning with the preceding diatonic (seven-tone) major and minor scales, pentatonics must lose two notes per octave. Sonically, pentatonics have a more aggressive or angular quality, sounding a bit less naturally melodic than their diatonic counterparts.

There is a major pentatonic and a minor pentatonic. To make a pentatonic, we start with a diatonic scale and cut out two notes—but which ones? The major scale loses its 4th and 7th. The minor drops its 2nd and ♭6th.

Track 30

Example 44 – **Pentatonics: Shedding Diatonic Tones**

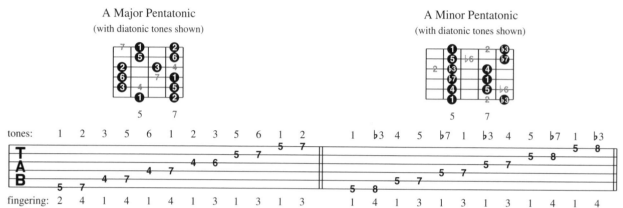

FYI: These pentatonic patterns are often called *boxes* because of their two-note-per-string shapes. That is, if you visually connect the outside "dots," different shaped boxes appear.

Of course, for our purposes, learning a pattern of dots is never enough! We want to learn these scales by their sound and tonal structure. So listen to each short melody on the CD, identify the tonal structure by ear, and write it down (answers on page 162). Finally, play each melody on the guitar as you sing along. Each fragment is played twice—once in each octave. (You can sing the same octave each time—whatever fits your vocal range best.) Although they look different in terms of their shape on the fretboard, musically they are identical (except for being an octave removed).

TIP: Sometimes string bending can blur the lines a bit regarding tonal structure, as a given note may begin on one tone and gradually rise to its higher, target pitch. If the pitch bend is fast, you can simply regard it as being the target pitch. If, however, it rises or falls slowly, you can notate it as one pitch bent to the next, as in 4 ⬆ 5.

Track 31

Example 45 – **Ear Training with Pentatonics**

    a) Root = A _____

    b) Root = A _____

    c) Root = A _____

    d) Root = A _____

    e) Root = A _____

    f) Root = G _____

    g) Root = B _____

    h) Root = F♯ _____

    i) Root = E _____

The *blues scale* is a minor pentatonic with an added ♭5th tone. This creates a chromatic series with the 4th–♭5th–5th. Below is the diagram, followed by some ear-training examples. It has all the angular aggressiveness of minor pentatonic but with the added interest of chromatic tension. (Answers on page 162).

Example 46 – **Ear Training with the Blues Scale**

Track 32

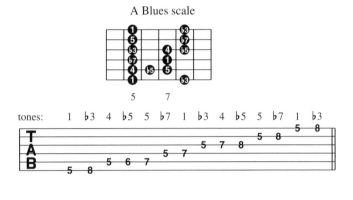

a) Root = A _____

b) Root = D _____

c) Root = A _____

Modes

Modes are *displaced* scales. For example, if you consider a scale's *second* note to be the root (instead of its first note) and play up from that point using all the same notes from the original scale, you are playing that scale's *second mode*. By definition then, modes always share the same notes as the parent scale. This is demonstrated below using G major as the parent scale.

Example 47 – **Modes of G major**

Track 33

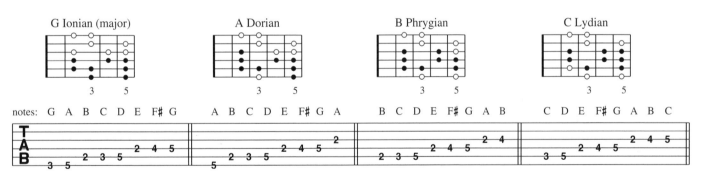

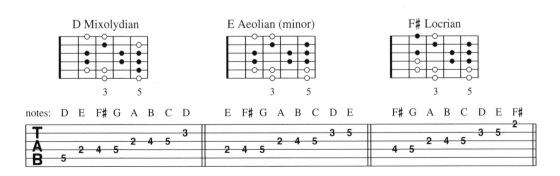

Below, these same modes are arranged so each shape is rooted on the sixth string—that is the only difference. Again, each of these patterns uses the notes of the "parent" scale (G major) exclusively.

Example 48 – **Modes of G major, Roots on string 6**

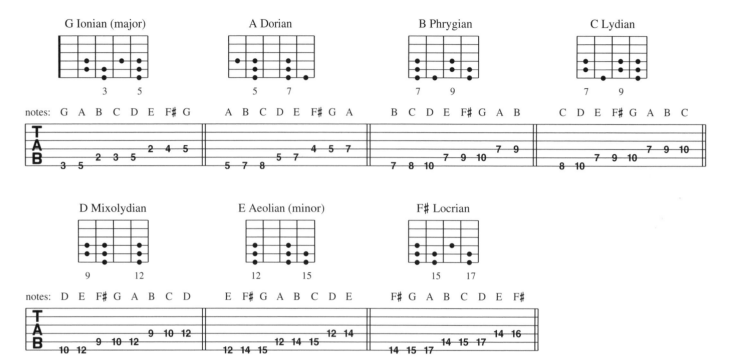

FYI: Since all the modes above share the same notes (G–A–B–C–D–E–F♯), we say they are "in the same family," or *related*. Relative scales and modes use the same notes, but have different roots.

Instead of looking at them as relatives, we can also drop them all to the same root note and compare them one to another as different scales in their own right. This is called viewing them in *parallel*, and it allows several advantages. For one thing, since they are no longer relatives, they'll probably get along better.

FYI: Parallel modes use the same roots, but have different notes.

On the following pages, the modes are viewed in parallel, all based on A. I have pointed out the unique qualities for each mode as a scale in its own right. Since we've already covered the major (Ionian) and minor (Aeolian) there are really only five new scales (modes) to consider. On the CD you'll hear a short melody using each mode. Listen to each melody as you follow along with the tonal numbers that are given. Then, using the mode shape and that "tone spelling," play each lick on your guitar. Transcriptions appear in the appendix.

TIP: Dorian and Phrygian are minor modes, sharing a minor 3rd tone. Notice the minor triad arpeggio "skeleton" in solid black within each of these scale patterns. The non-triad tones are in grey.

Example 49 – **Ear Training with Modes**

Dorian mode

1–2–♭3–4–5–6–♭7
Easy access: Minor scale with a major 6th
Quality: Minor feel with a bright spot in the upper tetrachord
Sample melody tones: 1-1-♭3-♭7-6 | 1-1-♭3-♭7-6-4 | 1-1-♭3-♭7-6 | ♭3-♭3-4

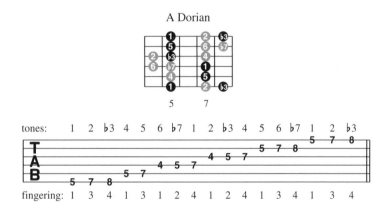

Phrygian mode

1–♭2–♭3–4–5–♭6–♭7
Easy access: Minor scale with a flatted 2nd
Quality: "Excessively minor," Spanish flavor with dramatic ♭2nd
Sample melody tones: 1-♭2-4-5-♭6-5-4-♭3-♭2-♭3-1 | 1-♭2-♭3-♭2-1-♭7-1-♭7 ↑ 1-♭7-♭6-♭7-♭6-5 | 4-♭3-♭2-1-1

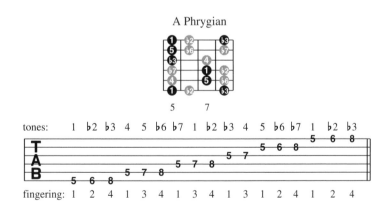

Lydian mode

1–2–3–#4–5–6–7

Easy access: Major scale with a sharped 4th

Quality: Lost, spacey, floating, airy, mystical-major

Sample melody tones: 1-2-3-#4-3-2-1 | 5-5-6-5-#4 | 1-2-3-#4-3-2-1 | 5-6-5-3-#4-5-6-7-#4

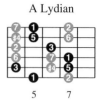
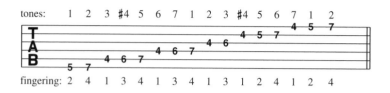

Mixolydian mode

1–2–3–4–5–6–♭7

Easy access: Major scale with a flatted 7th

Quality: Major's easy-going brother, no triumphant resolution

Sample melody tones: 1-3-4-5-4-3-1 | 3-1-♭7-♭7 | ♭7-6-1-6 | 6-5-1-5 |
1-3-4-5-4-3-3 | 1-♭7-2-♭7 | ♭7-6-1-6-1 | 6-5-1-5

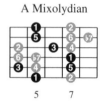
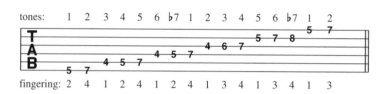

TIP: Lydian and Mixolydian are major modes, sharing a major 3rd tone. Look for the familiar major triad arpeggio shapes in black. Locrian includes a diminished triad.

Locrian mode

1–♭2–♭3–4–♭5–♭6–♭7

Easy access: Phrygian mode with a flatted 5th

Quality: Diminished flavor, darker than minor

Sample melody tones: 1-1-1-♭5 | 4-♭5-♭3-4-♭2-♭3

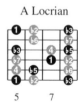
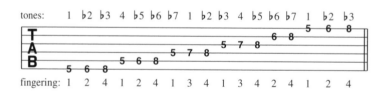

FYI: The Locrian sample melody includes power chord 5ths on a portion of the melody, making in essence a "melody of 5ths." Technically, the A5 tonic chord includes E♮(5) which is not in the A Locrian mode. Still, you get the gist of a Locrian feel here by virtue of the Locrian melody within the root movement of each power chord.

TIP: These modes can be difficult to memorize because the patterns are similar to one another in places. A good way to help burn these shapes into your brain is demonstrated in CD track 35. Start with the lowest note of a scale, go up one note, and then back down. Then move up two notes and back down—then three, four, five, etc. With each repetition you add only one higher note to the pattern. Try this on all the previous modal shapes.

Now let's clear up a little modal confusion. If modes use the same notes as their parent major scale, why do they produce such completely different qualities? They certainly don't sound major. The answer is that a scale's (mode's) quality has nothing to do with its letter-named pitches, or to whom it happens to be a relative. It's all about the relationship of each tone to its root. When you change the *root*, you change everything. Each mode can be seen as a scale in its own right and treated as such.

But if modes are scales, why not call them scales? Well, that's a throwback to the fact that they were created from a parent scale. So at least in terminology they remain second-class citizens. Major and minor occupy the "power seats," so to speak, and modes are the newcomers to the block. Seems that music terminology is always steeped in the past, looking backwards. But does that mean that you, as an artist, need to view them as having secondary importance? Not at all. **Modes are scales.** There it is, in print. Now maybe modes can start getting some respect.

Before moving on, make sure you have each mode and its tonal structure firmly etched in your mind, so you don't confuse them with the scales that follow.

Harmonic Minor & Phrygian-Dominant

The *harmonic minor* scale is a natural minor scale with a major 7th tone in place of the naturally occurring minor 7th. Check out the single-string patterns for natural minor and harmonic minor.

Example 50 – **Natural Minor vs. Harmonic Minor**

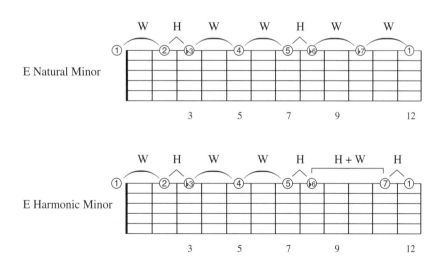

Notice that when the 7th is raised, a peculiar structure emerges: a minor third (technically an augmented 2nd), or three-fret interval appears between the b6 and 7, flanked on either side by half steps. This is the distinguishing melodic characteristic of harmonic minor, and it catches the ear with somewhat of a twist that you can hear in the following example.

Learn the harmonic minor shape below and listen to the two ear training examples. Identify the tonal structures by ear and write them in. (Answers on page 162.) Then play the examples on your guitar and transcribe them. Full transcriptions are in the Appendix to check your work.

Example 51 – **Ear Training with Harmonic Minor**

Track 36

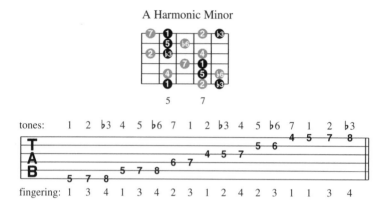

a) root = A_____
b) root = E_____

The *Phrygian-dominant* scale is very similar to harmonic minor. In fact it's a mode of harmonic minor, so it shares the same characteristics to a degree. Here the unique structure of a minor 3rd flanked by half steps appears in the lower tetra-chord (tones 1-4) instead of the upper tetra-chord (tones 5-8) as in harmonic minor. The main functional difference between them is that while harmonic minor is a minor scale type (with a minor 3rd), Phrygian-dominant—despite its overall dark feel—actually has a major 3rd. This gives it a distinct moment of "brightness" and more power than the standard Phrygian mode.

Learn the Phrygian-dominant shape below and listen to the two ear training examples. Identify the tonal structures by ear and write them in. (Answers on page 162.)

Example 52 – **Ear Training with Phrygian-Dominant**

Track 37

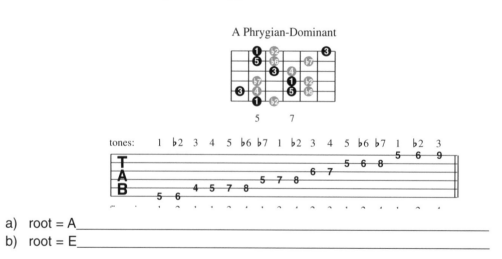

a) root = A_____
b) root = E_____

FYI: Phrygian-dominant is characteristic of Middle-Eastern and Moorish-influenced ethnic music. It is the same as the Phrygian mode, except with the brighter major 3rd. The dominant 7th arpeggio (1–3–5–♭7) appears naturally within the scale, which is the reason the name includes that term "dominant."

Jazz Melodic Minor

The "proper," or classical, melodic minor scale actually has a different structure in the ascending and descending forms. We'll cover why this is so at a later point. Here we want to consider the version of the scale called *jazz melodic minor*, which fixes the same structure for both ascending and descending. It is a minor scale with a major 6th and major 7th. In other words, the lower tetra-chord is that of a minor scale, while the upper tetra-chord is that of a major scale. To this author it seems to have a bit of a split personality—just can't decide which way to go.

Learn the jazz melodic minor shape below and listen to the ear training example. Identify the tonal structure by ear and write it in. (Answer on page 162.)

 Example 53 – **Jazz Melodic Minor**

Track 38

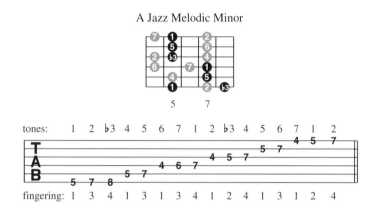

a) Root = A _____

Parallel Scale Exercises

Turn on a metronome to a moderate speed and play through any scale in an improvised fashion using steady eighth notes. Periodically, call out a new scale name and switch immediately to that new scale, regardless of where you are in the pattern and without missing a beat! Listen to the demonstration examples in CD track 39, then try it yourself. Although this may seem very difficult at first, I encourage you to persevere. It will pay big dividends.

 Example 54 – **Parallel Scale Exercise I**

Track 39

> TIP: Begin with just two or three different scale types to choose from. You may want to write them down so you can see the names as you play, in order to help remember your options. Gradually add more scales to the list, switching between them randomly and at random moments.

Here are all the scales, modes, and arpeggios we've covered, laid out on a single string. This enables you to truly compare each musical structure in its purest form. Notice how each structure on the left side shares a major 3rd (major family), while those on the right side share a minor 3rd (minor family). Play up and down each one until memorized. When you have that much down, try continuing each scale all the way up the fretboard (past fret 12). Also play them on other strings and move each pattern up the neck to various starting points other than open.

Example 55 – **Parallel Scales/Modes/Triads on a Single String**

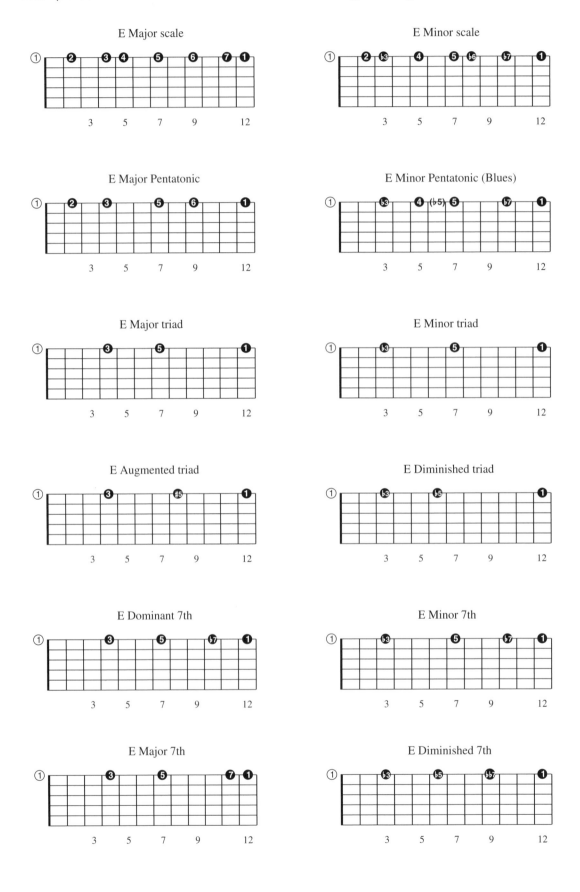

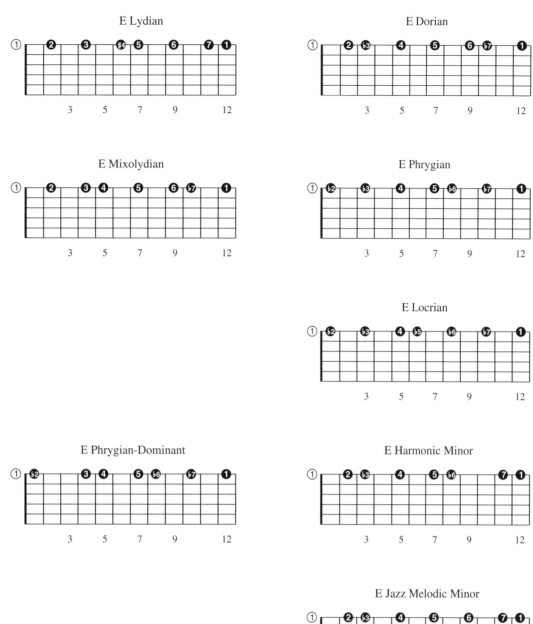

Now we will apply the idea from Parallel Scale Exercise I with each scale/mode/arpeggio on a single string. Three-note sequences work better for this one, as it keeps the position shifts more regular, but you can try improvising if you like. The fingerings are entirely up to you.

Example 56 – **Parallel Scale Exercise II**

Track 40

TIP: If you get a momentary "brain freeze" and suddenly draw a blank for the correct pattern of the new scale, that's okay. Just hold the note and wait until you can visualize the new shape—however long that takes—then continue on!

PART III: The Structure of Music

Here we move a step closer to real music and begin to see the various musical structures in action. Since application to music requires specific examples, certain styles of music will emerge. But the goal is not to catalogue every musical style in detail—that would require a thousand pages. We seek to establish a general framework. Then you will have the tools you need to analyze and fully understand those specific situations that interest you most.

From Scales to Keys

The difference between a *scale* and a *key* is the difference between *theory* and *music*. A scale is a theoretical construct formed by analyzing the pitches used in music, extracting them and stacking them up in order from low to high. A *key*, on the other hand, is the available set of tones that appear in the music itself. It's a subtle but important distinction, as we will see in a moment.

> FYI: Keys are scales in action. The key of C major, for example, is the musical setting in which C is the tonal center and the music is seen to most commonly use the pitches found within the C major scale.

First, consider that the *root* of a scale corresponds to the *tonal center* in music. A root and a tonal center are not the same thing, however. In a scale, the root is generally the first note—and the lowest note—played. In real music, the tonal center may not be the first note nor lowest note played. The tonal center is the central pitch toward which the music gravitates, or wants to "settle on." It is home base. The tonal center is determined by the sound of the music itself in the natural ebb and flow of its cadences.

What's the significance of this? Plenty. Many guitarists become confused about keys precisely because they fail to appreciate this distinction. They mistakenly conclude that when they play the *shape and position* of a G major pattern they learned, that they are playing in the key of G major—without further consideration of the musical context. This is not correct. Remember the modes? Families of modes all share the same notes. So the determining factor for a key cannot simply be the pattern of notes on the fretboard. The tonal center must always be considered first. *The key is the combination of the notes you play and what you play them over.*

The bass note will often shed light on tonal center. Over different bass notes, the same scale pattern may be heard as a different scale because the tonal center is different. The example below demonstrates this. Both the G major and A Dorian patterns are heard as G major when the tonal center happens to be G. Change the tonal center to A, and both patterns are now A Dorian.

 Example 57 - **G major and A Dorian Melodies**

Track 41

Listen to example 57 and you will hear the differing qualities of G major and A Dorian as clear as night and day. So the quality, or mood, has nothing to do with which pattern is used. In this case, it is entirely a matter of tonal center.

FYI: The patterns in Example 48 [G major, A Dorian, B Phrygian, C Lydian, D Mixolydian, E minor (Aeolian), and F♯ Locrian] can all be seen as G major. They could also all be A Dorian, or B Phrygian, or C Lydian, or D Mixolydian, or E minor (Aeolian), or F♯ Locrian. This does not mean that these different keys are the same—far from it! They all sound totally different. The correct key name for any given situation is determined by first locating the tonal center and then relating the notes to that reference point. The G major shape played over an A tonal center, for example, isn't G major at all; it's really A Dorian, and continuing to call it G major or see it as G major is wrongheaded! Shape alone does not determine a mode.

Now let's consider the musical staff and the issue of key signatures briefly. A *key signature* is the set of flats or sharps that define a particular key (or scale). If you move the major scale shape around the neck to various different positions, some interesting note patterns appear. The key of C major has no sharps or flats (C–D–E–F–G–A–B). G major has one sharp (G–A–B–C–D–E–F♯), D major has two sharps (D–E–F♯–G–A–B–C♯), A major has three sharps (A–B–C♯–D–E–F♯–G♯), E major has four sharps (E–F♯–G♯–A–B–C♯–D♯), and so on. The order in which the key signatures appear forms something we call the *circle of fifths*. Moving clockwise, from C to G rises a 5th, G up to D is a 5th, D up to A is a 5th, etc.

After E comes B, with five sharps, then F♯ with six. This is *enharmonically equivalent* to G♭ (with six flats), which means the two keys are spelled differently but use all the same pitches. The 5ths continue all the way around through the flat keys back to C. You don't have to memorize every detail here. Just look over the circle, noticing this pattern of 5ths, and the curiously increasing sharps and flats.

Example 58 – **Key Signatures in Circle of 5ths**

FYI: Move clockwise around the circle, and each key center rises a 5th. Move counterclockwise, and each key center falls a 5th (or rises a 4th).

The beauty of the key signature system on the musical staff is that once it is in place, *any* pitch dropped anywhere on the staff is automatically conformed to the scale/key. For example, below are several major scales shown on the staff with their appropriate key signatures. By pulling the sharps or flats out of the staff and putting them on the left side near the clef, the music looks a bit cleaner. Play each scale and write in the correct key. (Answer on page 162.)

Example 59 – **Key Signatures and Scales**

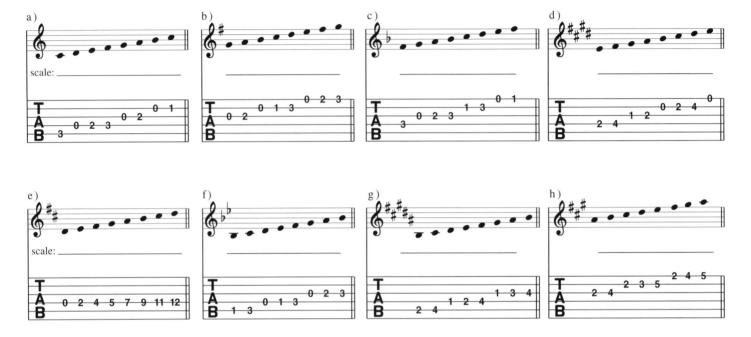

TIP: A nice fringe benefit of the key signature system when used in actual written notation is that any accidentals (sharps, flats, or naturals within the music) inform you that you have temporarily gone outside of the original key.

You may have noticed that key signatures themselves are entirely silent on the issue of tonal center. So in fact, key signatures don't define just the notes of major keys, they actually define entire families of related keys—that is, they define a major key plus its relative minor key, as well as five other related modal keys. You must look at the music and determine the tonal center, which in combination with the key signature will shed light on the key.

Since we tend to give the major and minor keys prominence over modal keys, there are in fact usually just two choices for each key signature. Following is a list of the major keys with their relative minors.

TIP: The relative minor is always found on the 6th step of the major scale. And the 6th step of the major scale is always a step and a half (three frets, or a minor 3rd interval) below the major root. Translation: You can always find the root of the relative minor down three frets from the root of the major. Going in reverse, from minor up to major, you have to move up three frets. The rule is: *relative major and minor are always three frets apart, and major is always higher.*

Example 60 – **Key Signatures: Relative Major and Minor**

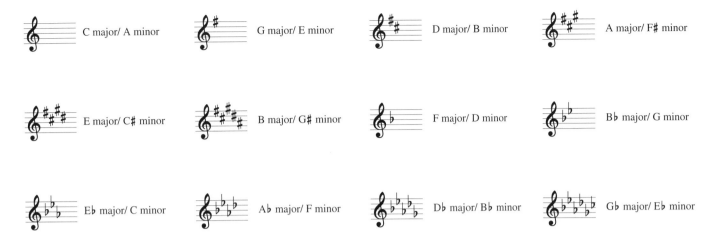

C major/ A minor   G major/ E minor   D major/ B minor   A major/ F# minor

E major/ C# minor   B major/ G# minor   F major/ D minor   Bb major/ G minor

Eb major/ C minor   Ab major/ F minor   Db major/ Bb minor   Gb major/ Eb minor

As you move ahead, you should have a handle on these primary points: 1) Tonal center is fundamental to key—not just the notes alone. 2) You should understand how the staff uses key signatures to define the available notes within a given key. 3) You should be familiar with some of the common key signatures.

Chords in a Key

Using only the notes within a given key, we may build chords upon each tone and thereby create a set of chords derived from that key. Let's walk through this procedure of building the set of chords in the key of C.

First, the C major scale is laid out on string 5. Then it is harmonized in 3rds, meaning that above each scale tone, a harmony note a 3rd higher has been added. Notice that some of these intervals turn out to be major 3rd shapes and others are minor 3rd shapes. Since there are no flats or sharps in the key signature, all the notes are *natural* to the key of C (meaning that they all dwell in that key). Then, we can add another "layer" of harmony by stacking another set of 3rd intervals on top of that. Relative to the original notes of C major on string 5, these are 5ths. At this point we have triads on each note of the C major scale.

Example 61 – **Harmonized C Major**

Track 42

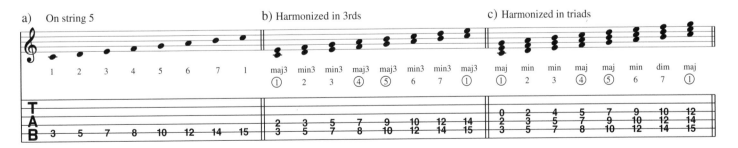

TIP: The steps that form major 3rds and major triads are 1, 4, and 5. These are circled above to help you see the symmetrical pattern that is formed. Steps 2, 3, 6, and 7 have minor 3rds, and step 7 also has a diminished 5th.

As guitarists, we don't often play triads like this. Here's what the chords look like played as full barre chords up the neck. We label these chords with Roman numerals to reflect their relationship to the tonal center. We use capital Roman numerals for chords with major 3rds (major chords) and lower case Roman numerals for chords with minor 3rds (minor chords). The diminished chord has both a minor 3rd (lower case) and gets an added "°" symbol to indicate that the 5th is also flatted. Notice that the C major scale is found in the root pattern of the chords below.

Track 43

Example 62 – **Chords in C Major**

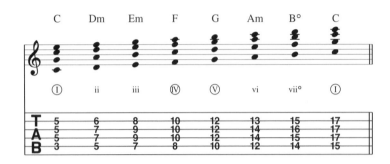

TIP: The I, IV, and V chords are the *primary chords* in the key and are major. The ii, iii, vi, and vii° are the *secondary chords.*

Remember, this derived chord pattern is generated by the major scale itself. So like the scale, it can also be shifted into other keys and the whole thing stays the same—it just sounds a little higher or lower depending on the starting pitch. Look for the major scale formula we learned earlier between the roots of the chords.

Example 63 – **Moving Chords into Other Keys**

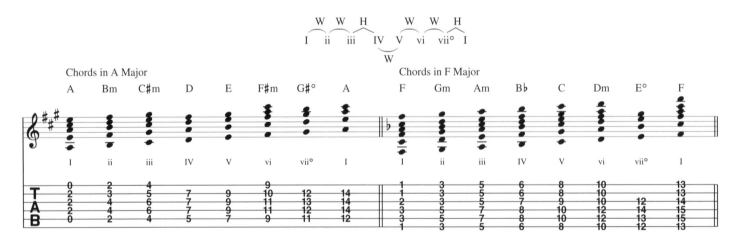

FYI: Chords are essentially just bigger, expanded versions of the single notes at their root. They impart a stronger and perhaps more "colorful" version of the root note.

Now go back and play the chord sequence for all the keys shown in the circle of fifths in example 58.

If we toss yet another harmony of 3rds on top of the triads, we create 7th chords. When harmonizing to 7ths, the chords I and IV become major 7th types, and V becomes a dominant 7th. The minor chords all become minor 7th chords, and the diminished chord becomes a minor 7♭5, or "half diminished 7th."

Example 64 – **C Major Harmonized to 7ths**

Track 44

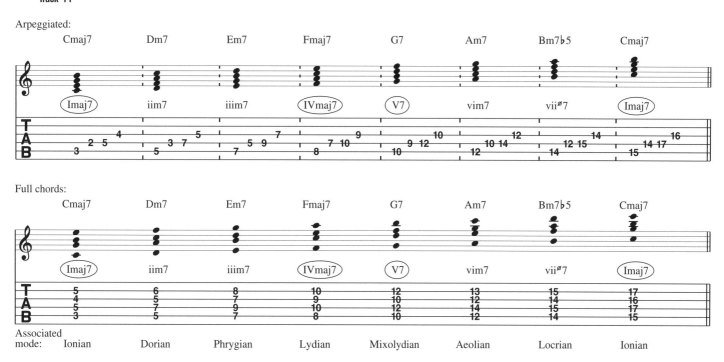

Associated
mode: Ionian   Dorian   Phrygian   Lydian   Mixolydian   Aeolian   Locrian   Ionian

TIP: The "associated mode" above can help you memorize each chord's unique flavor in the harmonized scale. For example, Ionian (I) and Lydian (IV) both contain the major 7th chord in their tones so they both harmonize to major 7th chords. Mixolydian (V) contains the dominant 7th chord. Dorian, Phrygian, and Aeolian each contain the minor 7th chords, and Locrian contains the half-diminished chord.

You can build up the minor key chord pattern by applying the same harmonization method to the natural minor scale. But we're going to use a shortcut. Remember that the relative minor scale begins on the 6th step of the major scale and uses the same notes. Therefore, the harmonized minor scale must also begin on major's 6th step and use the same notes and chords. When we change to the relative minor tonal center, the Roman numerals are simply renumbered to reflect the new tonal center as "i".

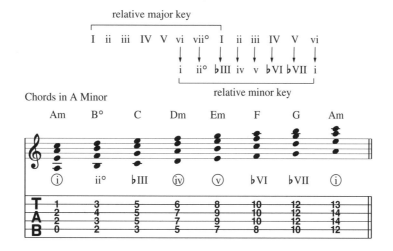

The primary chords in a minor key are i, iv, v, while the secondary chords are ii°, ♭III, ♭VI, ♭VII.

Basic Chord Resolution

As you recall from the section on Melodic Tendency, some notes sat comfortably where they were, while others demanded to move. Well, chords are no different—their behavior can be seen as a composite of the single notes that compose them. Chords that are uncomfortable, or tense, want to move toward stable chords. This motion is called *chord resolution*, and a progression of chords that resolve, or come to rest, forms a *cadence*.

It all revolves around the I (or i) chord. It is king of the hill and quite happy to sit idly on its throne. The chord built on the tonal center is also called, appropriately, the *tonic chord*. In a major key it is a major chord (I); in a minor key it is a minor chord (i).

The opposing force is the V chord, also called the *dominant*—presumably because its pull was heard to "dominate" any chord sequence. The V chord is considered to be sonically the "furthest away" from the tonic chord, and to have the strongest pull to it. Why? Look at its components. The V chord's tones (1-3-5) are 5-7-2 in relation to the keynote. If you recall, the 2nd and 7th tones pulled the strongest to the tonal center. No surprise then, that working together, they compel the V chord to resolve to the tonic. This resolution is called the *dominant cadence* or authentic *cadence* in classical music theory.

> FYI: Viewing each note as an independent *voice*, as below, harkens back to the time when music was primarily sung in the church and each tone was literally a voice. Considering each "voice" as it moves independently through chord resolutions is called *voice leading*. Notes may rise (leading tones), fall (leaning tones), or remain constant (common tones).

In the case of the basic V–I resolution, the root of the V chord can be heard to either fall or rise to the root of the tonic. In the upper portion of the chord, V's root acts as a common tone with the 5th of the I chord. The 3rd of V is the 7th tone relative to the tonic and rises strongly to it. The 5th of V is the 2nd tone relative to the tonic and can either rise to the 3rd or fall to the tonic. Only the first form of each of the following resolutions is demonstrated on CD track 45. But play all of them.

Example 66a – **The V–I Resolution**

Track 45

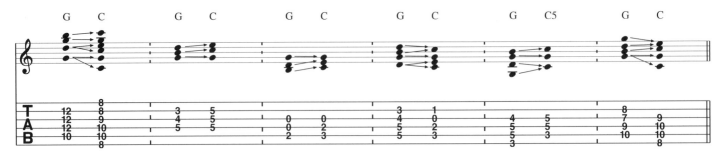

The pull toward resolution is further intensified if the V chord is harmonized to a 7th (add another 3rd on top of its 5th). The ♭7th tone of the V7 chord is the 4th tone relative to the tonic. So the V7 chord contains an additional non-chord tone that also demands resolution—the 4th wants to fall to the tonic's 3rd. Hence, the intensification of the pull.

Example 66b – **The V7–I Resolution**

Track 45 (0:07)

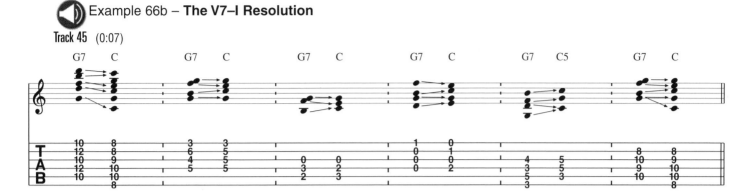

The IV chord is called the *subdominant* in classical music theory, as it was generally used to precede the dominant chord and basically "ramp up" to it. (Subdominant simply means "below" the dominant.)

Example 66c – **The IV–V–I Resolution**

Track 45 (0:14)

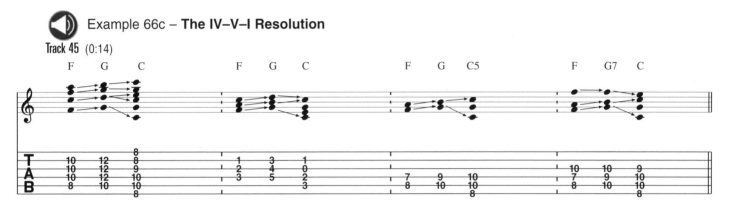

Alternatively the IV chord could also fall directly to the I chord, but doing so sounds more permissive than mandatory. Listen to the less demanding resolution of IV–I.

FYI: The IV–I resolution is known in classical theory terms as a *plagal cadence*, but it's also known as the "Amen" cadence due to its familiar use at the close of so many church hymns. Apparently the "soft" feeling of the IV–I was in tune with the idea of submission and the acceptance of divine will they were seeking to convey.

Example 66d – **The IV–I Resolution**

Track 45 (0:20)

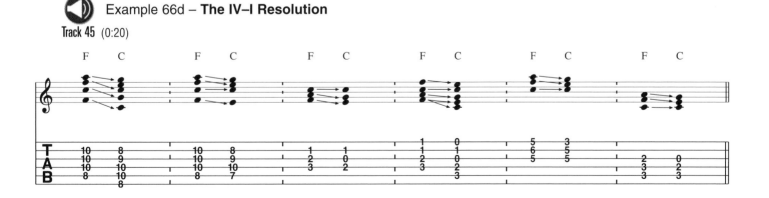

Now let's look at these chord moves in action. Following is a standard 12-bar blues progression. It starts with a long phrase on I, which establishes the tonal center. The second phrase moves up to IV and falls back again to I in the second phrase (IV–I resolution). The third phrase rises up to the "high point" (V), then winds back to I via IV. In the last measure we have a quick leap back up to V7 for the final turnaround moment, then we are dropped back to I to start again (V–I resolution). Harmonically, the 12-bar blues progression can be seen to be an ever-increasing build of resolutions. Listen for these familiar qualities as you play it.

Example 66e – **12 Bar Blues**

Chord Progression Ear Training

Tonality refers to the tonal center (e.g. "E") as well as the type of key that is built upon it (e.g., "major"). And as you know at this point, tonality not only includes a series of individual notes, but also a set of chords. Furthermore, you have learned that the notes and chords have particular motives, or tendencies. All this information is part of tonality. That's the theoretical side.

Now let's consider actual music. When chords appear in sequences within a song, we call it a *chord progression*. The progression defines a tonal center; chords move away from it temporarily and then return, move away and return again, in cycles. Furthermore, the progression serves as a "base" underneath a melody, giving that melody greater strength and purpose. Progressions and melody together define the tonality. But here we will concern ourselves only with the progression aspect. Melody will be added later.

Following are some chord progression ear-training exercises using just primary chords. First, listen and identify the tonic chord. Perhaps the best way to determine the tonic is to ask yourself, "If this chord were sustained at the end of the progression, would it make the most comfortable ending in a song?" If so, it's the tonic chord. Then identify the rest of the chords in the progression by ear, relative to that tonic chord. Write down the Roman numeral sequence you identify in the spaces provided. (Answers on page 162.)

Finally, learn each example by ear and play it on your guitar. Then write them out (transcribe them) on some blank staff/tab paper. Correct transcriptions for each progression appear in the Appendix to check your work.

Track 46

Example 67 – **Ear Training with Primary Chord Progressions**

a) _____

b) _____

c) _____

d) _____

e) _____

f) _____

g) _____

> TIP: There are some melodic embellishments in example 67, but they don't really change the bottom-line progression. For example, 67d adds blues-styled comping to the basic I chord, then we see an open tonic note (E) temporarily added over the V chord (B). Example 67f adds a quick suspended 4th over the first chord, and 67g inserts a melody and some open string common tones. Decorations like this may or may not be labeled. Here we are after the general thrust of the progression.

The secondary chords in a major key are ii, iii, vi, and vii°. When a power chord is used (no 3rd), you can optionally add a "5" after the Roman numeral to indicate it is a root-5th only. Still, the Roman numeral system shows you whether the *implied 3rd* is major or minor. That is, if the 3rd *were* played, what would the key suggest it be? Write in the Roman numeral chord sequence, learn the progressions by ear, and transcribe them onto blank staff/tab. Answers are on page 162, and full staff/tab is in the Appendix.

> TIP: We are looking for the significant chord motions here. If a chord is played momentarily, we may note its appearance, but it is not a "full member" of the progression. Likewise, passing notes may be ignored for our purposes. Also, notice the more delicate quality of the secondary, minor chords within the otherwise major sound of the key overall. You can use this cue to help identify them as secondary chords. Another method is to listen to the root of the chord in question and locate its correct scale step relative to the tonal center.

Track 47

Example 68 – **Ear Training with Secondary Chords**

a) _____

b) _____

c) _____

d) _____

e) _____

f) _____

Example 69 shows a few common minor key progressions. Identify the tonic and progression by ear, then write out the example and compare your work to the staff/tab shown in the Appendix. You may notice that the primary chords iv and v (minor) in a minor key are sometimes altered to IV and V (major). In cases where a power chord is used on iv or v, make the assumption that the chords are natural to the key (i.e., iv5 and v5—not IV5 and V5). (Answers on page 162.)

TIP: Listen for root movement. That is, boil each chord down to its root, and listen for the "melody" of these notes; it will shed light on the progression.

Track 48

Example 69 – **Ear Training with Minor Key Progressions**

a) _____

b) _____

c) _____

d) _____

e) _____

f) _____

g) _____

h) _____

Notice the strength of the major chords (♭III, ♭VI, ♭VII) in a minor key. Minor progressions that utilize these chords prominently (as opposed to the primary chords) are sometimes called Aeolian cadences. This includes many common rock progressions.

These days we are surrounded by music—radio, TV, movies, commercials, in the grocery store, the workplace, etc. Take these opportunities to practice identifying all the progressions you hear. It doesn't matter what kind of music it is. If there is no guitar line (which should be a prosecutable offense), listen for the bass line, as it often sheds light on the root movement.

The Story of IV–V–i...

Did you notice those major IV and V chords in the previous minor key progressions? How does that happen? Well, all the way back to the 1600s, composers noticed that the minor resolution of v-i was weak. (It lacks the half step pull of the major 7th scale degree up to the tonic.) So the minor v chord was altered to a major V chord, thereby creating a more powerful and satisfying V–i cadence. How do we change v to V? We must raise the chord's minor 3rd a half step. Well, this 3rd happens to be the 7th relative to the keynote, so raising it to major means we are in fact raising the 7th step of the key to major. And what is a minor scale with a raised (major) 7th? It was called *harmonic minor* because it is a *minor* scale altered for *harmonic* purposes. (Specifically, the purpose of creating a V–i harmonic resolution.)

Trouble appeared, however, when iv preceded V—at least trouble to early 17th century ears. In terms of the scale tones, the 3rd of the iv chord is the 6th step relative to the keynote. So a chord change of iv–V meant the possibility of making a melodic leap from ♭6 to 7 (W+H), and that was too "extreme" for the time. Therefore it became common to force iv major as well, giving us IV–V–i. Now we have a minor key with IV–V both major chords, which translates into a minor scale with both a major 6th and major 7th. (The major 6th step relative to the tonic is the major 3rd of the IV chord; the major 7th step relative to the tonic is the major 3rd of the V chord.) And thus, the *melodic minor* scale is born—so-named because the rise from 6 to 7 gives a more "melodic" sound. No such alteration was deemed necessary on the descending side, because classical music never dared to move from V down to IV. Hence, we have the different ascending and descending variations of the classical melodic minor scale. Of course, modern ears are no longer hung up on little harmonic issues like V–IV moves—all harmonic motions are fair game. So we can assign the classical melodic minor scale to the great trash bin of history—or at least to those trying to live entirely in the past (i.e., the real classical guitarists among us).

Inversion

When a note other than the root of a chord is in the bass position (i.e., the lowest note of the chord), we have an *inversion* of the chord. Below, a simple triad is shown in each of its three possible presentations: root position, first inversion, and second inversion. If second inversion is inverted again, we are back to root position an octave higher.

Example 70a – **Triad Inversions**

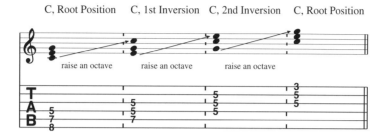

The voicing of the top portion of a chord may change without changing the inversion. Look to the bass note of a chord to define its presentation. Here are several common inverted chord shapes, played next to those chords in root position. Listen for the telltale characteristic of each inversion.

TIP: Inversions are often written as slash chords. For example C/E (pronounced "C over E") means you have a C chord with E in the bass. Since E is C's major 3rd, the chord C/E is in fact a C major first inversion. There are in fact three correct names for this chord: C/E, C first inversion, or C with E in the bass. They all mean exactly the same thing.

Example 70b – **Common Inverted Chord Shapes**

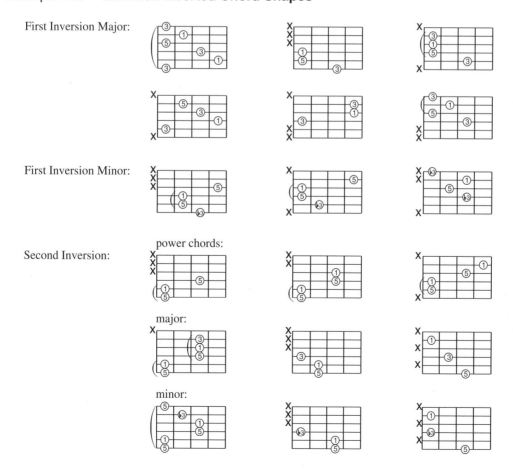

Now let's put some of these inverted chords into progressions. Write out the Roman numerals as before, but this time we will add a notation for the inversions. When the tonic appears with its 3rd in the bass (first inversion), write: I₃. When the 5th is in the bass (second inversion) write: I₅. (Note: This isn't the same as I5, a power chord.) Notating inversions like this is not standard practice, but it will do for our purposes here. Answers are on page 162, and staff/tab is in the Appendix.

Track 49

Example 71 – **Ear Training Progressions with Inversions**

a) _____

b) _____

c) _____

d) _____

e) _____

Riffs, Drones and Pedal Tones

A *riff* is a short, repeated, and structurally significant phrase used in a song. Riffs are most commonly two measures in length and may consist of single notes, chords, or a combination of both. Even though they may contain chords, however, a riff doesn't usually act like a progression because the notes move by too fast to really "sink in" and create any harmonic motion. Because of this, we say a riff creates a *static tonality*. When a riff repeats, there is no real "progression" because it doesn't "progress" anywhere. It simply vamps on a single, implied chord.

The riff below basically adds up to an Em7 chord, harmonically speaking. It is more art than science, but basically, we consider all the notes, weigh their relative importance, and try to match them up to the most accurate yet common chord—within reason. We don't have to account for every passing tone. Example 72a includes 1–4–5–♭7 in measures 1 and 3, and 1–♭3–4–5 in measures 2 and 4. So the whole riff uses all the E minor pentatonic tones: 1–♭3–4–5–♭7. The Em7 chord is very close (1–♭3–5–♭7). You could also simply label it "Em."

Track 50

Example 72a – **Riff Creating Static Harmony**

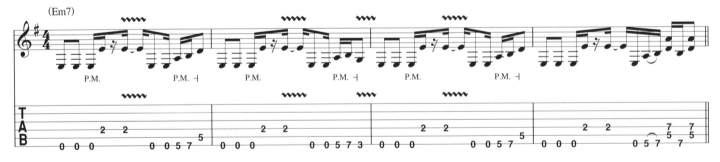

FYI: Technically, a repeating phrase in music is called *ostinato*. The word "riff" came from the blues, appearing first as a corrupted version of "refrain."

TIP: Riffs are commonly structured in one of several different ways: simple repetition (AAAA), a form with alternating endings (ABAB or ABAC), or a form with an ending tag variation (AAAB). Example 72a above could be viewed as an ABAC form with each letter corresponding to one measure. Of course these letters (ABC) don't have anything to do with pitch or chords. They are structural variables used to represent short musical ideas—much like the Xs and Ys in algebra that can represent any value.

The difference between a riff and a progression is largely one of size and scope. Perhaps this is most obvious when we consider that a riff can be moved *through* a progression. The following riff uses the E blues scale for four measures, then the A blues scale for two measures, and then moves back to E. The chord progression in a general sense would be best assessed as Em-Am-Em, or i-iv-i—the first eight bars of a 12-bar minor blues progression.

Example 72b –**Riff Moved Through a Progression**

Track 50 (0:14)

So a riff can be seen to sustain the harmony in an abstract or figurative sense. Now if we *literally* sustain the tonic note within the music for a long period of time, we have what's called a *drone*. This is common to eastern Indian music in particular. In Western music, the *pedal tone* is a closely related idea. But it is usually not sustained as long as a drone. A pedal tone is a pitch that is sustained under a chord change. It is as if one element of a chord (usually in the bass) is sustained against a temporary chord change. Then, often, the chord that changed may move back to "rejoin" the pedal tone.

FYI: The term *pedal tone* originated in organ music, where the lowest bass notes were played by the feet with pedals.

Example 73 begins with a sustaining pedal tone in the open low E string. After four measures, it changes to a palm-muted pedal tone. That is, the pedal tone is played intermittently in between the chord changes.

FYI: The pedal tone below is contained within the guitar part. But it can also occur between instruments. For example, the bass guitar could sustain the tonic underneath guitar chord changes, creating a different quality of pedal tone.

Example 73 – **Pedal Tone and Palm-Muted Pedal Tone**

Track 51

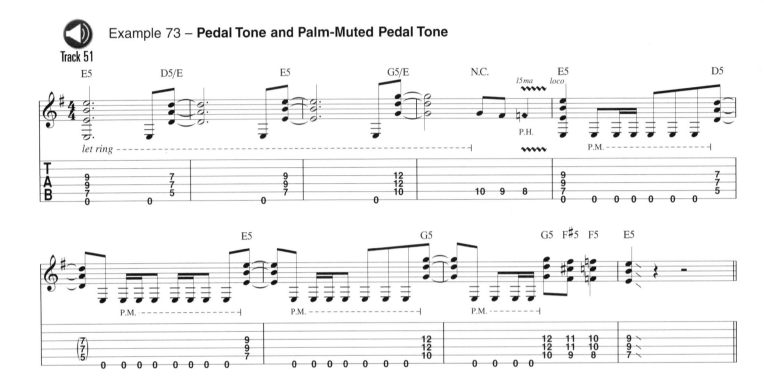

Example 73 is also a good example of the fact that not all chords in a progression are equal, harmonically. Here we have a minor progression (i-♭VII-i-♭III) with an ending tag that walks down chromatically to F5 (♭II). This ending moment, however, goes by fast and doesn't really rise to the same level of importance as the general chord motion. So while we can be aware of the presence of this tag, we should realize that it's not a full member of the progression in a harmonically significant way. It simply marks the end of the phrase and "colors" it with a ♭II moment.

Riffs and progressions are different things for sure. They create different stylistic effects and they interact differently with regard to melody. But there is a point where the two concepts meet. Is it a fast progression, or a riff with chords? You may find situations where the line seems to blur, but in most cases it is easily discernable.

FYI: Relying on static riffs in song structure tends to push the music toward the heavier styles of rock and metal. Moving them through I–IV–V progressions lends a blues quality. On the other hand, progressions working together with melody tend to sound more naturally "melodic." You'll find this approach at the heart of pop, top 40, and mainstream rock.

Now learn and analyze the harmonic content of at least a dozen riffs of your choice.

Parallel, Modal and Blended Tonalities

Within progressions, you are never "locked into" using just the set of chords diatonic to the key. Progressions can often be seen to borrow from *parallel tonalities*. A parallel tonality is another type of key based on the same tonal center. So the parallel minor of A is Am; the parallel major of Em is E, etc.

Play the following progressions and notice the subtle "twisting" of the ear when it suddenly pulls from the parallel key. You could think of this as being a very quick, temporary key change. But the keynote doesn't change; only the type of key changes.

Example 74 – **Progressions with Parallel Major/Minor Chords**

Track 52

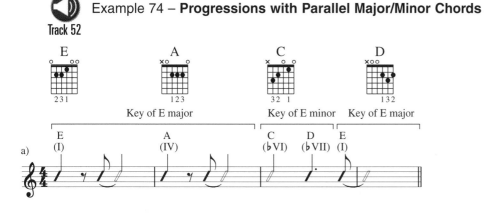

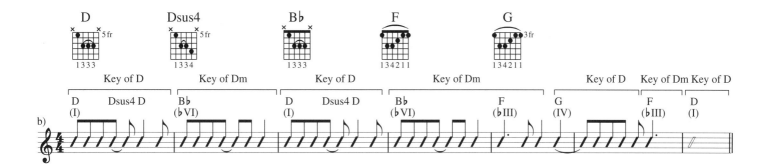

In minor keys, it is fairly common to substitute a major tonic chord. But is this really a minor key with a moment of brightness on I, or is it a major key that turns minor when it leaves I? Sometimes there is no clear answer if the chords are fairly evenly divided. (Is a zebra black with white stripes or white with black stripes?)

Although major or minor are generally at the basis of a key, it is possible that any mode may be granted that "heightened" status. When a mode is at the heart of the key, it is known as a *modal tonality*. Below are the harmonized chord sets for the Dorian, Phrygian, Lydian, Mixolydian, and Locrian modes.

TIP: It may look very complex, but it's not as bad as it seems. Realize that the chord sequence for each mode is exactly the same as that of the parent major scale. The only difference in each is the starting point and therefore, the Roman numeral numbering of each chord. Memorizing all this is optional. Having a general understanding of what is happening here, however, is mandatory. So play through enough of this until it starts to make sense.

Example 75 — **Modal Keys**

Songs rarely use the chords of a mode exclusively because modes tend to sound somewhat "unsatisfactory" as a key. They don't provide a strong enough sense of finality on the tonic. So it doesn't feel as though the chords really "come to rest" or naturally gravitate toward the modal tonic. Yes, we can force it to do so, but we are fighting an uphill battle. Indeed you undoubtedly noticed this already as you played through the previous modal chord sets—you just don't feel too "right" when you stop on the tonic. And sounding a bit "unmusical" in that regard makes them somewhat more difficult to learn.

By contrast, both major and minor make a pretty good case for their respective tonics. Simply play the chord set up or down and, if you just follow your ear, it will guide you to rest upon either the major or minor tonic. Therefore, it is far more common to see music draw upon a mode in a mixed way, blending it with standard major or minor. These "amalgam keys" could be called *blended tonalities*.

Look at the three chord sets below. If you examine the roots of each chord you will see a mode underlying each set. But notice that the harmony is not the true modal harmony (as on the previous page). Instead, we really just have one prominent chord from the modal key blended into an otherwise major or minor key.

TIP: Even though there is only one chord from the modal tonality, the influence of that mode is very strong here because the root movement lays out the mode clearly and without contradiction. (A contradiction only exists within the harmony.)

Example 76 – **Blended Chord Sets**

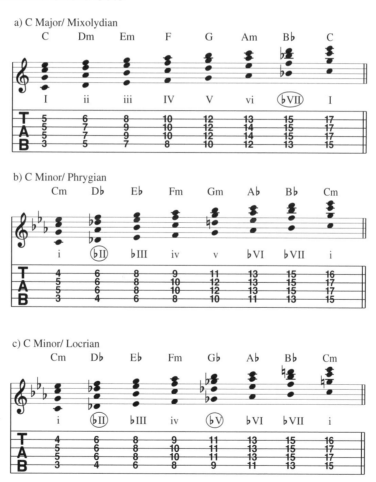

FYI: The first blended tonality below, Major/Mixolydian, may in fact be more common in rock and pop than the true major key itself. It allows for the typical "major-ish" chord progression bVII–IV–I. The other minor tonalities have appeared in rock and metal. Others exist as well. You could easily create all sorts of far-out, blended keys of your own with a little imagination. But would they be useful and sound good? Who knows?

Here are a few progressions that use these blended modal/major/minor tonalities. Identify the Roman numeral sequence by ear and fill in the blank. Answers are on page 162. Then transcribe the examples. To check your work, staff/tab notation for each progression appears in the Appendix.

Track 53

Example 77 – **Ear Training with Blended Tonalities**

a) _____

b) _____

c) _____

d) _____

e) _____

All the progression examples presented so far have only been enough to introduce the important concepts. To gain a thorough working knowledge and fully develop your ear, you will need to see many more examples in action. So take a moment to analyze the chord progressions for each song you learn and notice what those relationships look like on the fretboard. Each specific "shape-relationship" you uncover is like a little snapshot. There are literally dozens of ways the same progression can appear on the fretboard, but after you piece together enough snapshots you will start to see the big picture. In fact, as you progress, music itself gradually seems more and more simple as the common threads tie together different songs and styles. Eventually no analysis is needed; it all becomes completely intuitive.

So pause now to analyze at least a dozen songs. If you need help making sense of anything, find someone qualified to help you. Then continue on with the next section.

Exercise 78 – **Analyze a dozen songs of your choice. Then do a dozen more!**

Advanced Resolution

The authentic (dominant) cadence actually may appear in a number of different incarnations. These advanced variations appear in classical and jazz primarily. If that's not your cup of tea, you probably don't have to memorize each of these in ten different places on the fretboard, but you should still play through these examples and get the gist of what is happening here. This will certainly help further develop your ear and give you a greater understanding of unstable tones generally. We will begin with the basic V7 to I pull, upon which all of the following are based.

Track 54

Example 79a – **The V7–I Resolution**

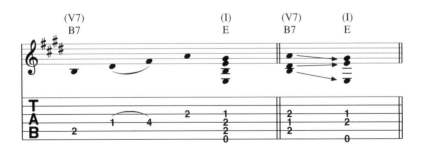

If we remove the root of the V7 chord (tones 5–7–2–4 relative to the keynote) we have the vii° chord (tones 7–2–4 relative to the keynote). This is particularly unstable and resolves strongly to the tonic. Since it is contained within V7, vii° is a "partial" V7—essentially another aspect of the same cadence.

Example 79b – **The vii°–I Resolution**

Track 54 (0:22)

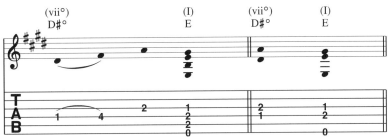

Stack another 3rd harmony on top of the 7th, and we create a 9th chord. Flat that 9th, and it pulls for an even stronger resolution to the tonic. A V7 chord with an added ♭9 is known as a V7♭9, consisting of the tones 5–7–2–4–♭6 relative to the keynote.

Example 79c – **The V7♭9–I Resolution**

Track 54 (0:40)

Now remove the root of V7♭9 and we are left with a fully diminished 7th chord (vii°7). In other words, V7♭9 and vii°7 are related to one another in exactly the same way that V7 and vii° are. In each case we have just stacked another 3rd harmony on top. Relative to the keynote, the tones are 7–2–4–♭6.

Example 79d – **The vii°7–I Resolution**

Track 54 (0:56)

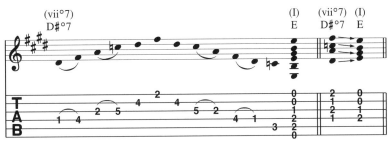

The *tritone substitute* (♭II7) is a more advanced variation. The ♭2nd tone (root of ♭II) is a tritone away from the 5th (root of V), and it also pulls strongly to resolve on the tonic. It is difficult to see how ♭II could possibly be any kind of V chord, but if you arpeggiate it and look at the tones, you'll see that a ♭II7 chord contains ♭2–4–♭6–7 (relative to the keynote). Look at the vii°7 previous and notice there's only one note different—the 2nd versus a ♭2nd, which simply moves it closer to the tonic and thereby strengthens the resolution even more. So ♭II7 is the slightly deformed half-brother of vii°7, who as we already know is a full, upstanding member of the dominant cadence family. The simple substitution rule is this: in place of a V7, try ♭II7 if you like.

Example 79e – **The ♭II7–I Resolution (Tritone Sub)**
Track 54   (1:10)

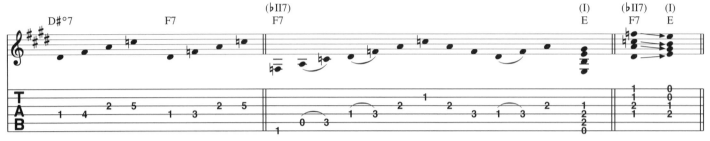

> TIP: All of these dominant cadences resolve equally well to a minor tonic chord (in a minor key).

The *half diminished* chord (vii°7), also known as the minor 7♭5 chord (m7♭5) also resolves to the tonic, similar to the fully diminished (vii°7)—except perhaps a little softer and more easy-going.

Example 79f – **The vii°7–I Resolution (vii7♭5)**
Track 54   (1:47)

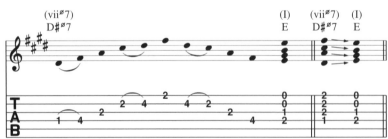

All these "pulling" chords share one thing: they are composed of unstable tones. To look at it another way, take the tonic chord's root, 3rd, and 5th (the stable tones) out of consideration for a moment. What is left? We have the major and minor 2nd, the perfect and augmented 4th, the major and minor 6th, and the major and minor 7th. Combine these in different sets and you can create all the dominant chord forms. (You may need a 5th here or there, but let's not nitpick.) This is easy to see on the following page. Write in the tones of each pitch relative to E in the space between the staff and tab. Answers on page 162.

> TIP: The main purpose here is to gain a sense of where these non-chord tones lie relative to the tonic chord's "arpeggio skeleton," and where they like to resolve. Then you have a tremendous insight into guiding melody, progressions, and solos.

Example 79g – **Unstable to Stable**

Track 54 (1:58)

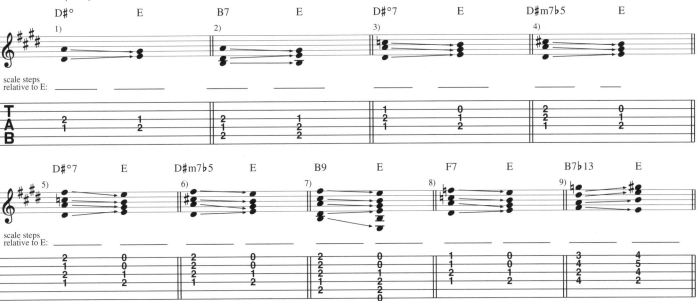

Knowing all the specific chord names is really optional in this author's opinion. It is the awareness of the resolutions of the individual notes within them that breathes life into your progressions and melodies. In fact, you can simply "make up" these unstable chords as needed in your own music. Simply gather a few non-chord tones from your key, and play them together. Let your ear guide you.

As an example of what I mean, here is the bridge section from my instrumental tune "Sunrise," (*Exottica*, 2000) in the key of E major. It plays off the dominant cadence with a drone on the tonic E. At the B7 chord, I've also forced the common tone E in on top as well, making it... well let's see... technically a B11/E. Then the second resolution introduces G♯, again pulled from the tonic chord E. Over the dominant (B) however, G♯ happens to be a 6th (13th) tone, so technically it forms a B13 chord. But it wasn't written by thinking about jazz chords; it was simply the result of following melody (as dictated by my own inner ear) and as a result fusing a portion of the tonic chord together with the V chord. The descending arpeggio sequence at the end functions to build an even stronger version of the same V–I idea, to "cap" the phrase.

Example 80 – **"Sunrise" Bridge (Authentic Cadence)**

Track 55

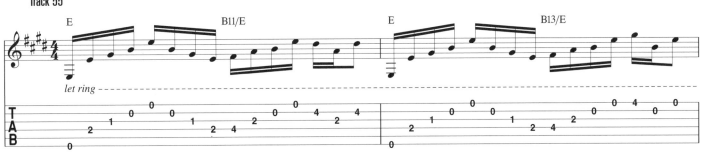

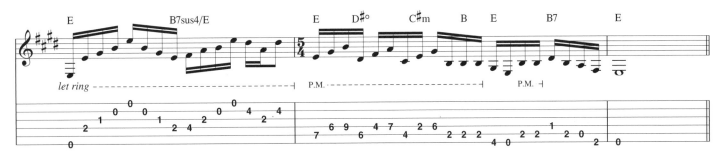

Resolution Strategies

A number of specific strategies evolved over time to wring out more musical ground from these various resolutions. The first was to stack up two or more resolutions back to back, creating a "V chord of the V chord." That is, the V chord of the V chord pulls to V, which then in turn pulls to the tonic. Since the V of V is actually II, this makes a II–V–I.

Play this sequence of chords in a few different keys and notice how it sounds. In a major key the naturally occurring ii chord is minor. So it may appear either minor (ii) or altered as a major (II) version. (Remember that V pulls better than v.) The II–V–I sequence is found in a wide variety of styles—from baroque to classical to jazz to pop. It can quickly get out of hand if you start substituting various advanced dominant resolutions for each V resolution (but only crazy jazz people get carried away with this sort of thing). Here is a standard ii–V–I with just a small bit of harmonic exploration.

Example 81 – **ii7–V7–Imaj7 Jazz Progression**

Track 56

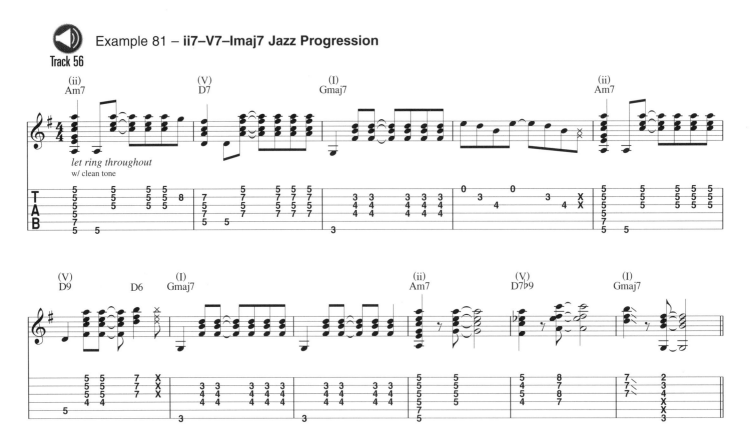

J. S. Bach's "March in G" is an example of a prominent V of V use in a different context. Here a motif is established in G. After three measures, we hit the V chord (D) in measure 4. This pulls back to the tonic to kick off measure 5. Next we shift to II7 (V of V) to set up a pull to V. As expected, we get to V in measure 7, where we have a quick shift back to II (A) to reinforce the following move back to V. Bach also inserts the common tone D over the A at the end of measure 7, creating a temporary Asus4. More specifically, the top voice anticipates the move to D, which is then confirmed by the bottom voice at beat 1 of measure 8. This creates a slight temporary harmonic dissonance and release to underscore and strengthen the chord resolution at measure 8.

If we look deeper, we can see chord motion outlined in every note. The opening note D is the V of G and pulls directly to it immediately. Then at the end of measure 1, we have F#/A (tones of D, or V) followed by G/B (tones of G, or I) and E/C (tones of C, or IV). So there is a mini V–I–IV, which then pulls into G of measure 2. Look through the remaining measures and identify the chord tones of each "skeletal" chord like this.

Track 57

Example 82 – **II–V–I ("March in G," J. S. Bach)**

*Left hand fingering
**fret w/ thumb

"half close"

FYI: Clearly, measure 9 is not the end of the piece, as you can guess just by listening. The section that follows returns to the main theme on G (not shown). However, the music does seem to come to a temporary rest as it pauses at measure 9. When the rhythm phrasing tells us we are closing a section, but we end on an unstable chord that begs to continue, we have something called a *half close*. (In this case, by ending on V, it's technically known as a *half cadence*.) By contrast, if you finish an ending phrase on the tonic chord, you have a *full close*. You can hear this same quality very often in modern music. When a progression completes a four- or eight-measure section on the tonic, it creates a full close. When the progression completes such a section and remains on an unresolved chord, which then resolves into a new section of music, it is a half close. Notice the end of any 12-bar blues progression. The "turn-around," or final measure, is on the V. This completes the phrase rhythmically, but harmonically it dumps us back into I to begin the whole thing again—a perfect example of a half close.

Another way the dominant can be employed is to create a cascading set of V chords. Below is an excerpt from Paganini's 5th Caprice for Violin, written in the late eighteenth century. In measure 3 you will find arpeggiated chords within each beat, creating the progression A–Dm–G7–C. Each is the dominant of the next, so A is the V of D, D is the V of G, G is the V of C.

Track 58

Example 83 – **Cascading Resolutions ("5th Caprice," N. Paganini)**

slight P.M.

Quick analysis: The one-measure motif contains a quick move to V7 in beat 2, worked into a stepwise ascent of the notes A, B, and C on the downbeats 1, 2, and 3. In measure 3 Paganini turns to A major on beat 1, then cascades through a set of V of V chords. Next comes a diminished arpeggio which at first appears to be a G#°7. However, while the next arpeggio does contain the note A, it is itself a diminished arpeggio which serves to pull us toward the overall V chord of the key, E, to end the four-measure phrase with a half close. Working backwards, the correct name of the diminished chord that pulls to E must be a half step below E, which is D#°7. And the diminished chord preceding that must likewise then be D°7. (Remember, the four notes of all fully diminished chords are equidistant, and therefore any can be considered the root. Composers could then play with this ambiguity by suggesting a target direction, and then surprising the listener with a last second, unexpected change.)

As we saw in example 75, sometimes the resolution may appear in stages, resolving the upper and lower portions of the chord separately—like turning a corner in two steps rather than one. Another way this can be done is with a *cadential six-four* chord. This is a quick I–V–I progression where the first I appears in second inversion. When it appears like this, instead of sounding like a tonic chord, the first I can be heard as a type of V chord with a suspended 6th and 4th. (Hence the "six-four" designation in the name.) These suspended tones then fall to the V chord's 5th and 3rd, which in turn makes a final dominant resolution back to I. The cadential six-four provides a kind of "slingshot" effect to amplify the V–I that follows. Notice the cliché classical sound it gives in this section of Paganini's 5th Caprice.

 Track 59   Example 84 – **Cadential Six-Four ("5th Caprice," N. Paganini)**

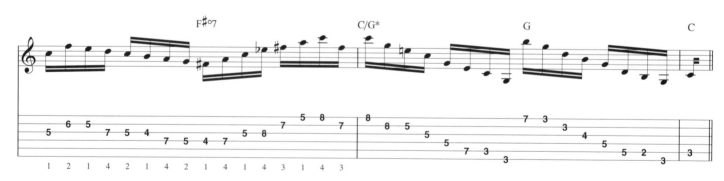

It is also possible to run two resolutions back to back, which both point to the same outcome, but *without* one pulling strongly into the next. So unlike previous examples where each chord fluidly pulls to the next, this is a situation where we are heading for one resolution, then the composer jumps to a different track, to attack the target chord from a new direction. For example, both ♭II and V pull to the tonic. But ♭II doesn't pull so much to V. Still, no one can argue the compelling nature of the ♭II–V7–i cadence as presented in Beethoven's 2nd movement of Piano Sonata #23. In theoretical terms, the ♭II chord in a ♭II–V move is known as a *Neapolitan chord*.

Example 85 – **Multiple Resolution, Single Target ("Appassionata," L. van Beethoven)**
Track 60

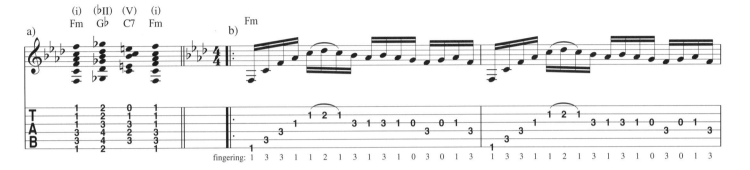

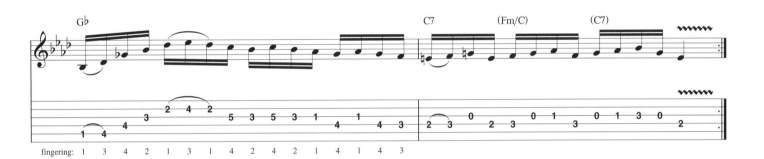

TIP: Notice the great care with which every note has been placed for its harmonic value. Notes falling on the beat have a slight natural emphasis to the listener. Look at how Beethoven winds the scale around to land on Fm chord tones on each downbeat within the theme, making it spell out 1–5–♭3–1. In measure 3, we see this emphasis given to chord tones of G♭, 3–5–3–1. Then in measure 4 we get E (3rd of C), F (hint at coming resolution), G (5th of C), and back to E (3rd).

Chord resolution was the primary propellant for much of the music from the Baroque and Classical periods. Today, chord resolution is still woven into the fabric, but the "rules" are greatly relaxed. In fact, many of the methods of harmonically "bucking the system" have come to characterize certain modern styles to such a point that our collective ears have grown accustomed to these "disturbances," and what once would have been unthinkable now sounds only quaintly cliché. However, in an effort to develop one's ear and recognize chord progressions by their sound and pull, it is very helpful to go "back in time" and listen carefully for these pivotal chord resolutions, sharpening your awareness of them. Even though the suggestions they offer for harmonic completion are no longer requirements (and can be ignored if you choose), studying them will help you more fully develop your ear.

Now that you've had this little trip back in time, let's bring your heightened awareness of resolution to some modern sounds. Listen for chord motion and resolution in every song you hear.

Melody Over Progressions

Melody works together with the underlying progression to create a whole that is more than the sum of the parts. The progression lends power and direction to a melody. It gives the melody more of a reason to move as it does, or it works to resist that movement. And the melody creates interest where the chord progression alone is relatively bland. The two working together create a powerful synergy.

Below is a simple melody over a progression of primary chords (I–IV–V). Notice how it basically hugs the chord tones (*harmonic tones*). The asterisks (*) mark points of intentional "disharmony," where the melody moves to a non-harmonic tone. These moments create a sort of melodic suspension. In the example below, the chords sound on the left stereo channel and the melody is on the right. You can dial your balance control to listen to the melody alone, then listen to both together and notice how the progression helps make it sound stronger and more purposeful.

> TIP: Many of the notes played in the sample melody move outside of the primary positional patterns we've covered for the E major scale. But by using the scale formulas and your knowledge of scale structure, you should be able to extend the scale as needed to see how every note is indeed found within the E major scale. For now, look at each of these "digressions" from the primary positional pattern as additional/alternative scale shape.

Example 86a –**Melodies over I–IV–I–V Major Progression**

Track 61

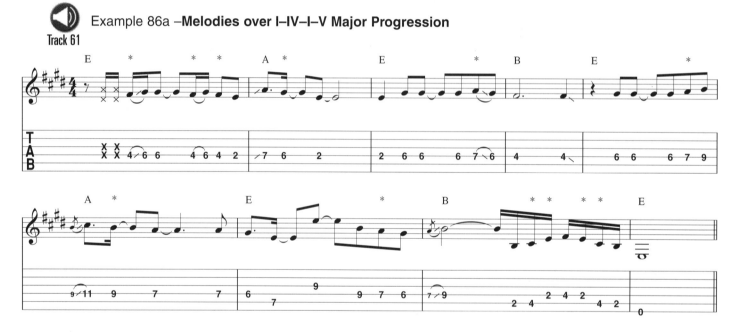

The diagram below shows which tones relative to the keynote are chord tones for each of the primary chords:

Chord:	Tones in Triads:	Tones in 7th Chords:
I	1–3–5	1–3–5–7
IV	1–4–6	1–3–4–6
V	2–5–7	2–4–5–7

> FYI: A melody note tends to sit at rest over the chord that contains it as a chord tone—even if the chord itself is "unstable" and wants to resolve. So you essentially have "pulls within pulls." For example, over the V chord you may have a non-chord tone, which creates a temporary suspension and pulls to the tones of the V chord. So the melody could resolve to one of the V chord's tones, but then that V chord tone itself pulls toward the tonic to resolve again, along with the V–I chord resolution.

Now turn your stereo's balance control to the left (chords) and play CD track 61a again, this time making up your own melodies. All the notes should be drawn from the E major scale, for now. Notice how it feels when you nail the chord tones over the right chord. It gives your melody a purposeful strength, as it feels somewhat "attached" to the chords. Then play with it by intentionally pulling away from the chord tones temporarily and returning to them. Also, you may want to simply listen to the chords a moment and allow your imagination to take over. What kind of melodies do you hear? Can you translate them onto the fretboard? Feel free to roam outside of the primary positional scale patterns using your knowledge of the E major scale structure (whole and half steps).

> TIP: Eventually all this will become second nature. The process is simply that you imagine melodies that sound good, and out they flow. However, at the beginning stages it helps to pay attention to some of these "technical" details and be aware of the exact chord tones you are using. Gradually you can and should trust your instincts more and more and go with them even if you don't fully understand what you are doing harmonically. Remember, the understanding is only here to help facilitate the *doing*. As the understanding fades into a subconscious process, let it go. That's exactly what we want!

Example 86b is a faster paced I–V–IV progression, also in E major. The sample melody I've played here is a melodic-style solo that uses a motif repeatedly—specifically, the three opening notes can be heard to recur over each chord similarly as it descends. Then the second time through (measures 5-8), it builds in the opposite direction, ascending. The third phrase (measures 9-12) is a busier, guitar lick-type approach that pays little attention to the underlying chords. The fourth phrase (measures 13-16) completely ignores the chords. Notice at that point how the same set of notes acquires a different sound when the chords move underneath.

 Example 86b –**Melodies over I–V–VI Major Progression**
Track 61 (0:36)

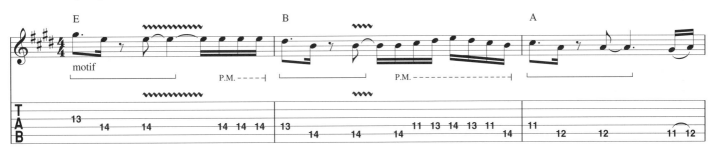

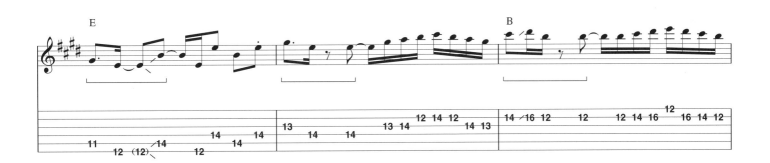

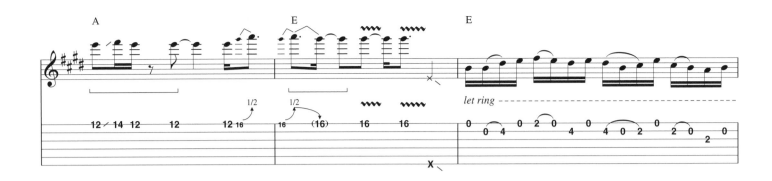

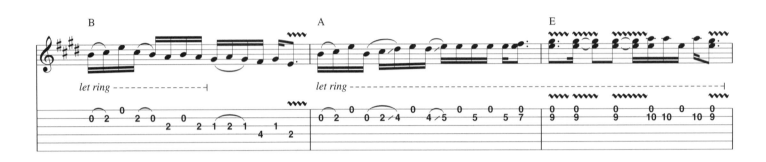

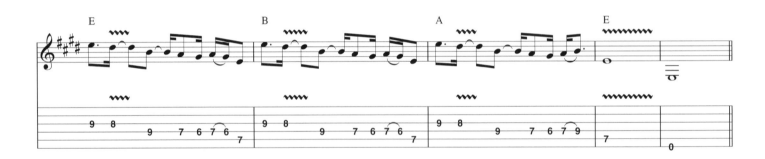

TIP: Vary your approach. Try long sustaining phrases, then try short rhythmic bits with breaks. Try sticking closely to the chord tones, then completely ignore them. And go everywhere in between. There are no rules here—just different approaches creating different results. Try playing short "vocal" type melodies, with lots of space. Try long, sustaining guitar-type melodies. Try building off a motif—melodic, rhythmic, or both.

TIP: A blues-inspired melodic technique is to begin sustaining a chord tone over the tonic, then hold it over the next chord where it is no longer a chord tone (creating tension), and finally allow the underlying chord to return to the tonic and relieve the tension. In other words, the melody becomes static while the underlying chord moves away and back. The tension/resolution in this case comes from the temporary conflict between melody note and underlying chord. Interestingly, this concept can be applied not only to a single note, but to a repeating motif, or even an entire phrase. Try it.

EXTRA CREDIT: Analyze every note of my solo in two ways. Write out the scale tones under each note relative to the tonal center (E), and to the underlying chord. So, for example, a D♯ over a B chord would be labelled 7 relative to E, but it is 3 relative to B.

FYI: Although they appear differently on the guitar, chords and single notes are not really so different. Chords are created from the scale tones, and all the tendencies inherent in the individual tones are represented collectively in the chords. Make it a habit to view not only each chord's relationship to the tonic, but also to see how each individual note of each chord relates to the keynote. With this approach, the line between chords and individual notes blurs and gradually disappears until eventually you don't play "chord shapes" as much as collections of multiple voice leading melodies. This gives you tremendous insight and powerful new options in creating music of your own. You are no longer stuck with given chord shapes. You are free to create your own voicings, as needed.

Just as we saw with progressions and riffs, some notes of a melody are more important than others. Basically, notes fall into either of two camps: either they are strong tones, that are harmonically significant, or they are embellishments, which serve to "decorate" the other more important tones. Below are a few simple examples of strong notes, or "target notes," and embellishments.

Example 87 – **Target Notes & Embellishments**

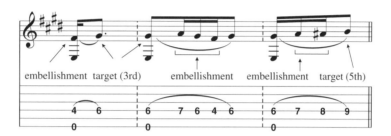

Embellishment and approach tones may even be altered or borrowed from outside the key. When this is done, these out of key notes don't affect the fundamental harmony significantly, although they may "color" the sound a bit differently than using only notes of the key (diatonic).

FYI: Non-harmonic tones actually have a variety of different names depending on how exactly they're used. These terms come from hard-core classical music theory:

- *Passing tone*: A non-harmonic scale tone that is played in transition between two different chord tones, often of the same chord.
- *Neighbor tone*: A non-harmonic tone that falls between two occurrences of the same chord tone. (There are upper neighbors and lower neighbors.)
- *Suspension*: A harmonic tone that is sustained, or repeated, over a following chord in which it is no longer a chord tone. The suspension may or may not resolve.
- *Appoggiatura*: A suspension without the preceding chord. In other words, a dissonant, non-harmonic tone that resolves into a harmonic tone.
- *Approach note*: A general term for any non-harmonic scale tone that precedes an important target note.
- *Altered Approach note*: When the approach note would be a whole step away from the target note (either above or below), it may be chromatically altered to be only a half step from the target note, thereby increasing its pull to that target note.

While it would make a nice theory test to correctly label all the notes in all the preceding examples as either passing tones, neighbor tones, suspensions, etc., this level of classification isn't fully necessary for the artist seeking to develop a mastery over melody. The important thing is that you recognize the harmonic and non-harmonic tones, and that you realize the effect this has. Then improvise your own melodies, "playing" with the melodic tensions as you like!

CD track 62 is a major progression in A, this time with secondary chords. Again the chords are on the left channel, and a sample melody is on the right. Turn your stereo's balance control to the left and try improvising melodies over this progression. Don't play fast! Savor the quality of each tone within each specific harmonic placement. Remember, each note will have an entirely different character when it appears over a different chord. Imagine that you are singing with your guitar, and play/sing melodies that could actually be vocal lines.

Track 62

Example 88 – **Making Melodies, Major Progression with Secondary Chords**

Chords:	With Basic Triads:	With 7th Chords:
ii	2–4–6	2–4–6–1
vi	1–3–6	1–3–5–6

74

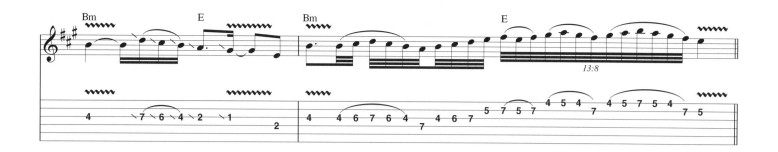

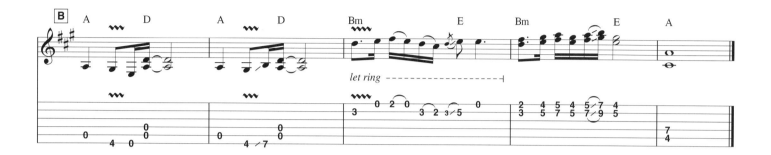

EXTRA CREDIT: Add the 7th tones and use them freely as chord tones. Listen for the color and stylistic change this brings to your melodies.

Now let's look at a minor context. Here is a minor key chart for the chords used in the example that follows. Look over the chord tone diagram in example 82, learn the sample melody I've played, and notice how the chord tones are used.

Example 89 – **Melodies Over i-♭VI-♭VII Minor Progression**

Track 63

Chords:	With Basic Triads:	With 7th Chords:
i	1–♭3–5	1–♭3–5–♭7
♭VI	1–♭3–♭6	1–♭3–5–♭6
♭VII	2–4–♭7	2–4–♭6–♭7

75

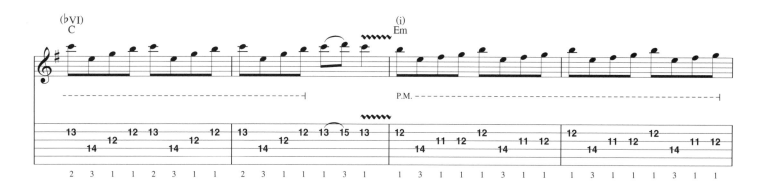

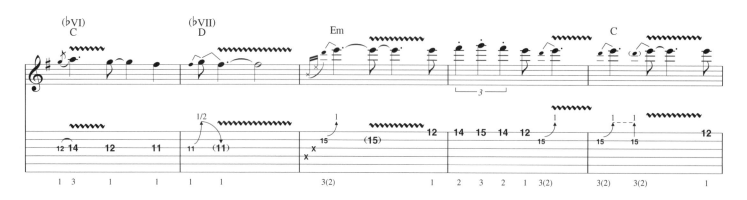

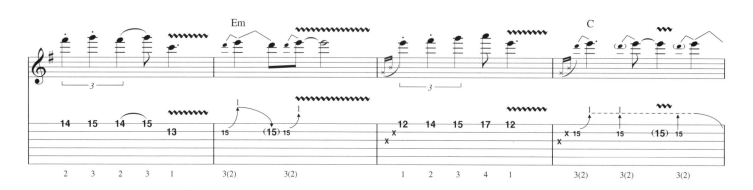

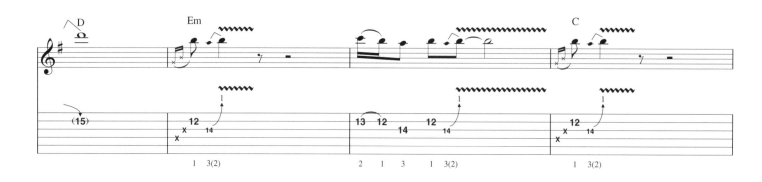

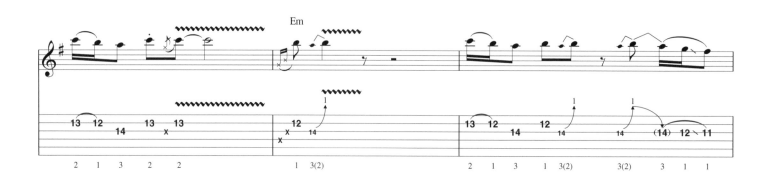

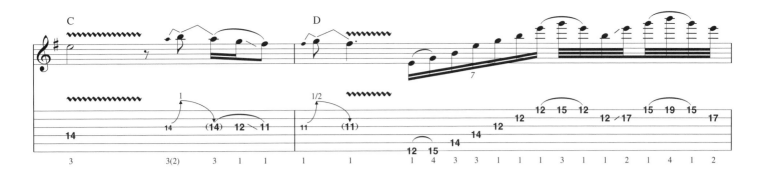

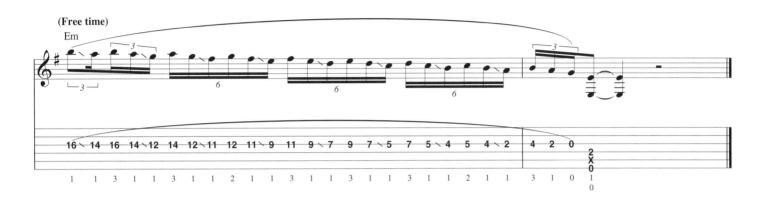

QUICK ANALYSIS: Over the first Em chord, look for G–E (♭3-1); then over the C chord it walks up to C–B–G (1–7–5) hinting at Cmaj7. Measures 5–8 repeat the basic idea down an octave, but end over the D chord on A (5). The next phrase begins an ostinato section. Notice how the first tone changes from B (over Em) to C (over C) and back. This phrase ends with F♯ (3) over D major.

The third eight-measure phrase begins at measure 17. Now it's in the upper register. The important note over Em is clearly E, with plenty of vibrato and rhythmic embellishment. Over C we repeat the focus on E, now C's major 3rd, but the phrase ends with a nod toward the C root (end of measure 20). On the return to Em (measures 21–22), we see another variation that climbs higher, to A (Em's 4th—not every significant tone has to be a chord tone). This phrase ends in measure 24 over D. The melody falls to D, the root.

The final eight-measure phrase utilizes open space. Over Em, we focus on B (5), building a new motif. Measure 26 is basically decoration, developing measure 25's new motif, and harmonically says "B" for the most part. Then over C in measures 27–28 we see it repeat. Now the B note makes it a Cmaj7, but the melody pulls up to C by the end of measure 28 to resolve. At the end of measure 32 there's a quick sweep in Em. Yes, it's over the D chord momentarily, but that's okay as it clearly heralds the impending end on Em. Then there's a quick descent down the Em scale to hit and resolve on the low root.

Did I compose this little melody thinking about all this? Not at all. I just played a few improvisations until I had a good feel for things I thought worked, then tracked it. Yes, I'm aware of the harmonic issues vaguely as I'm playing, feeling the pulls and resolutions of chord tones, but it's mostly a subconscious process. Eventually, that's how it will feel for you as well. But to get there it helps to see how it all works in detail first.

TIP: Instead of memorizing the scale tones that go with each chord as above, another way to easily see all the chord tones of any underlying chord is simply to superimpose that chord's arpeggio against the notes of the key. So for example 89, over the tonic chord you may see the Em arpeggio as chord tones. Then over the ♭VI chord (C) look for the C major arpeggio tones within the E natural minor scale.

Now it's your turn. Set the balance control hard left and create some minor melodies over the minor chord progression on CD track 63. As you do this, savor the color of each note you play—if you play too fast, you will miss the point of playing melody! Sure, for variety, go ahead and throw in some faster runs and licks, etc. But be sure to slow down from time to time and really draw upon the harmonic component in your melody.

The previous examples have all been standard diatonic progressions. But sometimes progressions change key or temporarily borrow from a parallel tonality. What happens then? Your melody/solo must change with it. The most obvious parallel tonality situation is when we see a chord that absolutely doesn't belong in the key. For example, if we are in E major, we may have a C (♭VI) chord. There is no C in E major at all, so we have clearly left the original key and are pulling from E minor. Your melody/solo needs to switch from E major to E minor over that C chord. (Now those parallel scale exercises are coming in handy!)

Yet the key shift may not always be so obvious. A more subtle method of borrowing from a parallel tonality is to shift the harmony only. Suppose we have a minor progression that includes a major IV or V chord as we saw in portions of example 69. Your melody/solo must account for this type of change. If you ignore this and try to play the ♭6th step of the key over a IV chord, for example, you're asking for a really sour note! Remember, IV means the 6th step of the key has turned major. (A major IV chord transforms a minor key into Dorian, a major V chord transforms it to harmonic minor, and both IV and V together make jazz melodic minor.)

Now if nothing in the progression contradicts your major 6th tone (from IV), you can simply use the Dorian mode throughout—the progression is in a Dorian modality. No borrowing is needed. But if there is a contradiction, it means you are borrowing between parallel tonalities. For example, suppose your progression also uses a ♭VI and/or ♭III chord (both of which contain the minor 6th step of the scale) in addition to IV. In that case you need to change between natural minor and Dorian. More specifically, you need to use the b6th over ♭VI and ♭III, and the major 6th over the IV chord. (Another option would be to avoid the whole issue and simply omit the 6th step entirely—play minor pentatonic and the whole issue becomes a moot point!)

What if the progression remains somewhat ambiguous about its tonality? Then you may define it harmonically as you choose—you can go "standard" or you can force it to borrow from a parallel tonality. In the following example, the opening progression is A5–C5–D5. The standard approach would be to regard it as i–♭III–iv. Since it's a minor key, you could play Am (or Am pentatonic or blues) throughout. But what if we turn iv into IV? Now we've got A Dorian over the IV chord, brightening things up a bit. And are we stuck with the implied Am tonic? Not at all. Why not force it to borrow temporarily here from A major and mix it up even more? The progression doesn't demand it, but it certainly allows the option. (Had the rhythm used a full Am chord, this wouldn't be an option.)

Example 90 –Melodies Over Progression with Parallel Tonality

Track 64

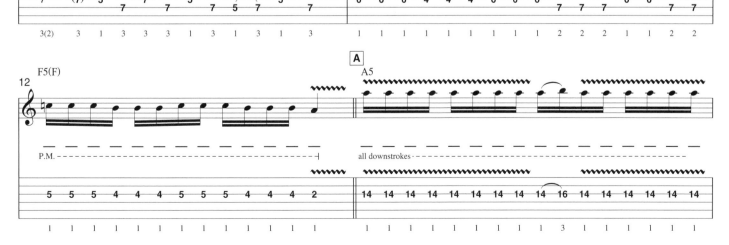

*Backing chord

**Composite tonality (melody with chords)

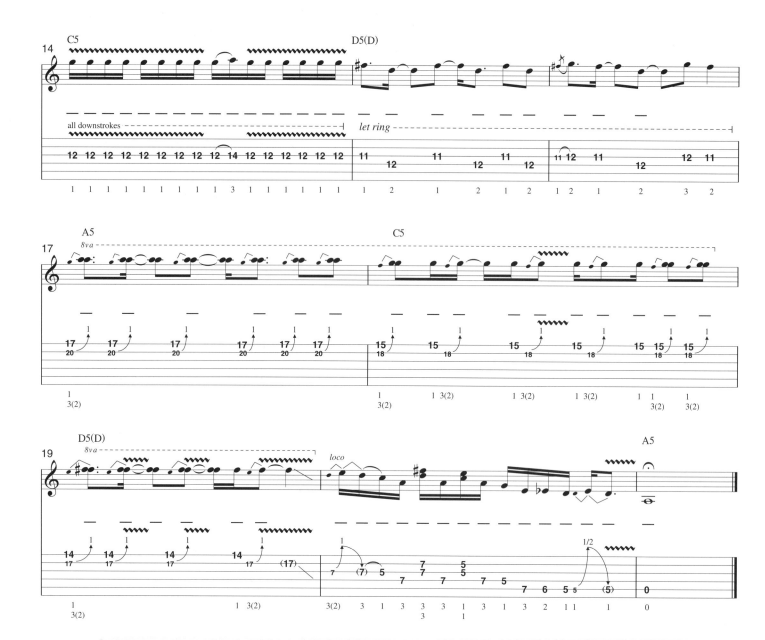

Quick Analysis: Notice the use of parallel major at measures 1, 5, and 11. Also, look for A Dorian over the D5 chords in measures 3–4, 7–8, and 20. For the B section at measure 9–10, I played straight A minor pentatonic over the first A5–F5, then went to the parallel major at measure 11. At measure 12 (over F5), I repeated the same scale steps and motif but back in the parallel minor so you can most easily hear the change in color. Upon the return to the A section beginning at measure 13, I chose to hammer out a very simple melody—A over A5, then G (5th) over C5, followed by F♯ (major 3rd) over D5. To help it not suck, the embellishment is accomplished by a slight finger vibrato and the use of all downstrokes, which gives it a bit more urgency. At measure 17, we go up an octave and try a different articulation—unison bends on the same A–G–F♯ melody.

Now go over the transcription and enter each note's tone relative to the keynote. (Answers on page 163.) Then circle all tones that are also chord tones of the underlying chord and notice the position of each note's "dual role" on the fretboard—both within the underlying chord's arpeggio shape *and* the scale of the overall key.

Next turn your stereo's balance knob hard left and make some melodies of your own over these chords. You can try staying in minor throughout (A natural minor, Am pentatonic/blues) and create a i–♭III–iv tonality, or make the I and/or IV chords major, or mix it up as you wish.

The plan in general is to follow the chord tones, but not too much. *Always* moving with the chords becomes tiresome. It is the surprises along the way that make life worth living, and melodies are no different. The art of melody is on some level balancing these subtle pulls and tensions, giving it some amount of predictability and familiarity without becoming too predictable or dull. You may follow the chord tones a little, a lot, or not at all. Sometimes, a strong melody or reappearing motif may completely "override" harmonic consideration.

In the end, after you learn and practice all this stuff, there comes a time to simply forget everything you know and just let your imagination take over—and listen. A detailed technical understanding of target notes, embellishments, approach notes, suspensions, etc., is not necessary to make great melodies and melodic solos. What you really want is to get a good feel for this generally and develop your ear to appreciate the subtle push and pull of chord tones in action. But realize at some point you have to "let go" and follow your ear. Great melodies are not created with a calculator!

TIP: Simple is usually better when it comes to melody—especially vocal melodies. Simple ideas are more accessible and usually have a wider appeal. And that brings up the concept of the "hook." A *hook* is an aspect of a song that has an interesting and memorable sound. Regarding melody, the hooks are often the short familiar resolutions paired with an interesting rhythmic presentation. But hooks are not only found in the melody. That's just one aspect of music. They may also be in the lyric, the backing music, any unique sounds or tones, or in the rhythmic foundation of the music. True songwriting magic happens when the right lyric, with the right shade of emotion, gets paired with the right melody that reinforces that emotion—then it all gets set into the right arrangement context, where its power can be fully realized.

Melody Over Riffs and Drones

Melody-making gets easier the simpler the progression becomes. And nothing is simpler than a one-chord "progression." Of course that is really not a progression at all, since it doesn't actually go anywhere. It is a *static harmony*. So you are effectively soloing over a sustaining tonic chord. That certainly makes the chord tones easier to follow! The only issue left to settle is to choose the correct type of key.

For that, identify the tones within the riff and determine what type of key it comprises. The fewer the tones in the riff, the wider your harmonic options are. (When the backing tones are ambiguous, you are free to define the key with your melody/solo.) Or to say it another way—you are free to use whatever tones you like, provided they do not directly clash against those within the backing riff/chord. Section A in example 91 takes place over a harmonically sparse riff that pegs only the root, ♭3rd, 5th, and ♭7th. And in fact, it is far more open than even this suggests. Almost the entire four-measure phrase rides on an E5 power chord (1–5). It only hits G5 (♭3–♭7) on the short ending tag.

TIP: Some of this solo is a bit quick (over the G5 section). If this seems out of reach or very challenging from a technical standpoint, pull out Speed Mechanics for Lead Guitar and apply the practice techniques found in Part II to iron out the trouble spots.

Example 91 – **Melody over Droning Riff ("Tao of Metal," from** *Metal Rhythm Guitar* **Volume 2)**

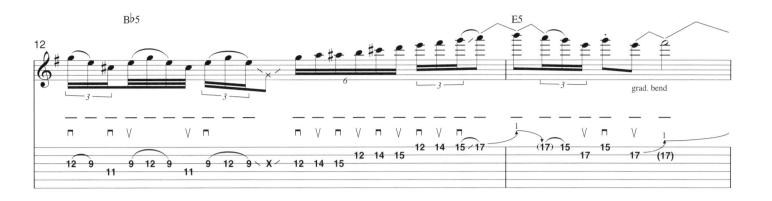

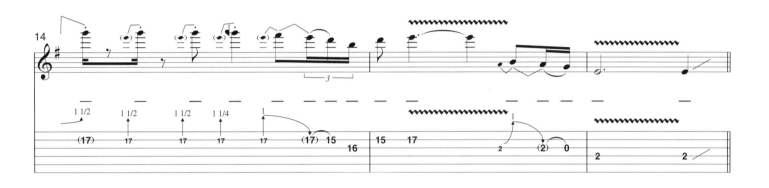

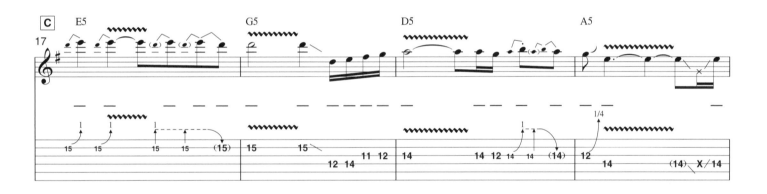

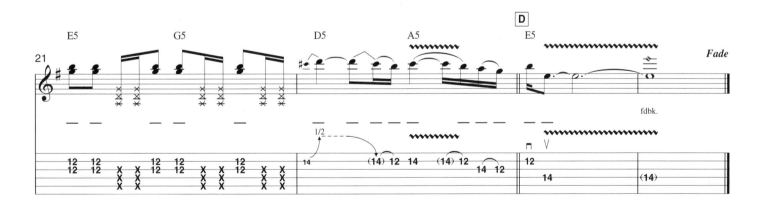

Learn this solo and then write in each tone relative to the keynote, again circling each tone that is a chord tone in the underlying chord. (Answers on page 163.) Then under each circled tone, write the tone relative to the underlying chord.

Quick Analysis: The melody here jumps up the tonic's arpeggio tones (1–5–♭7) and then hangs on the 4th. Measures 3–4 begin to repeat the opening two-measure phrase, except this time it comes down Em pentatonic and lands on the root. Remember tension-resolution? First we hang on 4 (unsettled "half close"), then we resolve the melody to 1. The B section is a solo moment over G5 (♭III), the relative major chord. Did I say to play only slow and melodic? Screw that. You've gotta dig in and rip! (I suggested earlier that you slow down because most guitarists can solo faster than they can really listen. By slowing down and learning how to really use the tones melodically, you gain a new set of insights and options. But after that is accomplished, you've got to wrap it all together with your best licks and runs... all options on the table!) I took the Em pentatonic/blues shape over G. Look for the G major chord tones (G–B–D, which are Em scale steps ♭3–5–♭7) at work within this section. After a long, contoured descent, we turn and come back up using the E diminished 7th arpeggio, then complete the ascent in measure 12 with a straight run up the combined E blues/Dorian scale (more on combined scales later).

Section C favors a melodic approach again with "filler" licks. Over E5, I'm on E (1). Over G5, I'm on D (5th). Then on D5, I run up to A (5th). A bluesy connecting lick then comes to rest on E (5th) over A5. Measures 21–22 condense the progression into two measures, and the melody obliges with G–B over both E5 (making ♭3–5) and G5 (making 1–3), D over D5, C♯ over A5 (making A major), and finally resolves to E5 with the notes B–E (5–1).

The rhythm section in example 92 just plays a simple tonic power chord, so there is literally nothing to contradict. You can play anything here—major, minor, any mode, any note you like! It's an open invitation for madness!

Example 92 – **Melody/Solo over Tonic Groove**
Track 66

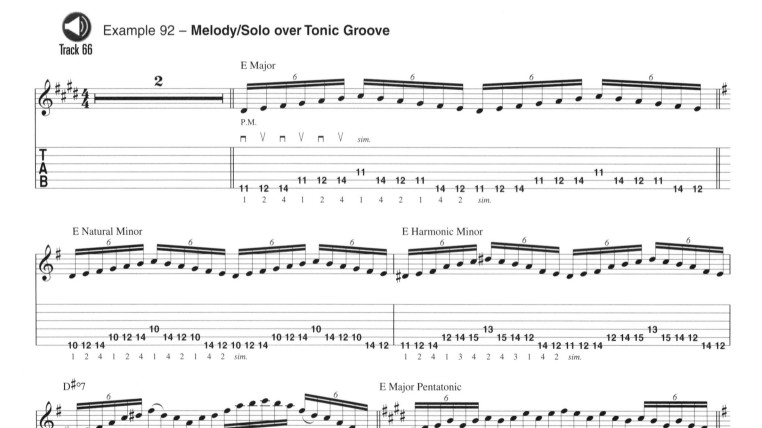

84

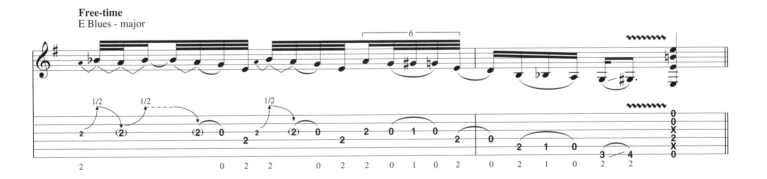

FYI: Tonality is a composite of the notes of all instruments. In the example above, the tonality shifts fluidly from major to natural minor, to harmonic minor (including a B7♭9—remember advanced dominant resolutions?), to major pentatonic, to minor pentatonic, to Mixolydian (specifically, a dominant 7th arpeggio), to an augmented tonality, and to a diminished 7th tonality. The closing descent moves chromatically to the final ending flourish—a minor pentatonic lick with added major 3rd. So, basically, it's all over the map. The only common denominator throughout is the tonal center. This is known as a *pitch axis* technique—shifting between parallel tonalities, with the tonal center acting as your axis.

Basically all the same principles that apply to melody also apply to soloing. The only real difference is that soloing tends to be faster. We'll go deeper into soloing over progressions in Part V. But for now, find or create some backing tracks to improvise melodies and melodic solos over. Or you can just play over songs. Analyze them first, so you know what keys you need to play in, and go for it!

Exercise 93 – **Buy, steal, or create a dozen backing tracks and "wax melodic"**

FYI: As we mentioned earlier, there is a point where riffs and progression come together. A fast progression can sound a lot like a riff. In terms of melody, just how long must a chord sustain before it exerts a significant pull upon the melody notes over it? The answer seems to be around two beats at a moderate tempo. Shorter than that and there seems to be little perceived interaction between chord and melody.

Harmony

Generally speaking, the word "harmony" refers to multiple pitches sounding simultaneously. So our study of chord progressions and their interaction with melody is in fact a study of *harmony*, or the *harmonic* aspect of music. But harmony also has a more specific meaning—a secondary melody line, or voice line, that moves along with the primary melody in order to help support and "thicken" it. Example 93 demonstrates a simple melody, then adds a harmony in 3rds, then a three-part harmony with 5ths.

 Example 94 – **Melody with Two- and Three-Part Harmony**
Track 67

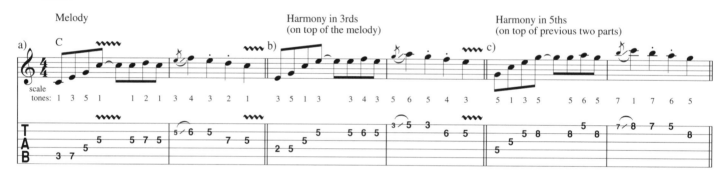

TIP: If the original melody begins on a root, the harmony (or second part) will begin on the 3rd, and the next harmony (or third part) will begin on the 5th. At times, other intervals will appear. In example 94, the melody climbs up the C major arpeggio. When it plays the second note (the major 3rd), the top harmony part moves to the root, making a 6th interval. Had it maintained 5ths, the harmony would have been playing the major 7th here instead of the root. This is perfectly doable if you like. It is a stylistic choice whether to use other harmonies or stick to the simple major/minor chords.

FYI: If this seems a lot like building chords in a key, you are right. Chords are nothing more than stacked up 3rds, just like these harmonies. So yes, you can see these harmonies as making chords out of each melody note. Extra credit: Identify each triad chord type.

EXTRA CREDIT: Identify each triad's chord type in 94c. Answers are on page 163.

Below is another approach to harmony, this time using 6th intervals. By going *down* a 6th, we arrive at the same pitch as going up a 3rd—it's just an octave lower. So we are still firmly on harmonically solid ground. Listen to the example, where the melody is first stated alone, then harmonized a 3rd above (not shown in the music). Then the harmony above is transposed down an octave to create the harmony in 6ths.

FYI: 3rds and 6ths are inversions of one another. An inverted major 3rd is a minor 6th, and an inverted minor 3rd is a major 6th. These are what's known as *complementary intervals*. Any two intervals that add up to an octave—major 2nd + minor 7th, perfect 4th + perfect 5th, major 6th + minor 3rd, etc.—are complementary.

 Example 95 – **Melody with Harmony in 6ths**

Track 68

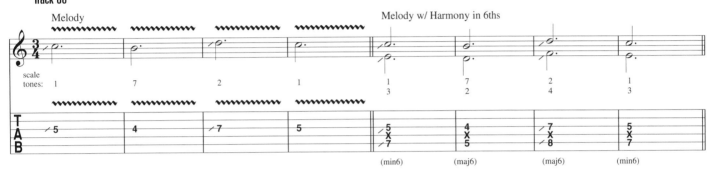

When melody centers around the 5th tone of the chord, adding a 3rd above that gives us 7th chords— a decidedly jazz flavor. You may want to do that, but more commonly (at least in rock and pop) you would try 6ths again. A 6th above the 5th is a 10th, which equals an octave plus a 3rd—so we are back to a triads again.

When the harmony moves in sync with the melody, as in all the examples above, it is called *parallel harmony*. That is, when the melody falls a step, the harmony falls a step. When the melody rises, the harmony rises. And when the melody skips a step, the harmony also skips a step, maintaining the same relative distance in terms of scale steps. To get a handle on parallel 6ths, try playing the C major scale harmonized in 6ths. Notice that the first set of 6ths in C major occurs between the 3rd and upper octave of each chord in the set, as in example 96a. Another set of 6ths is also hiding in the same chords, between the 5th and a 3rd above it, as in example 96b.

Example 96 – **C Major Harmonized in 6ths**

Track 69

TIP: Each set of 6ths can be seen to simply climb the seven chords in the key of C major. But since the third note of each triad is missing, we are in a sense implying its presence. What if we inserted a different 3rd tone to complete each chord? Then the same two notes could in fact be different chords. Some common alternative choices are shown in parentheses. What other alternative chords can you find? How many alternative choices are there if you don't constrain yourself to C major, but open it up to all parallel tonalities? You may find some interesting chord motions. Write a few progressions based on these and solo over them!

Harmony doesn't have to move in parallel. It can move in the opposite direction (*contrary motion*) or one voice can hold steady while the other moves (*oblique motion*). How does that work? It's just like voice leading with chords. Make a case for the harmony as if it were a melody in its own right, making sure it makes sense with the progression and doesn't clash too badly against the melody. Even 2nds are okay in some cases (for example, one voice holding the root and another climbing or falling to a ♭7th).

This is just the tip of the iceberg. You now have the basic tools to understand harmony, but in order to gain full facility with it you will need to see a lot more examples in action. So if harmony is important to you, you know the drill! Find specific harmony lines in songs that matter to you and figure out what they are doing. Learn and analyze the progression and the melody. Then look at the harmony and relate that to the melody and progression. After a dozen or so examples, you'll pretty much have it down.

PART IV: Fusing the Fretboard

At this point you know the function of all the tones and their organization in the common musical structures—within the primary positional shape at least. We also went beyond the primary position occasionally, but not in any systematic way. Now we will extend your knowledge into the remaining areas of the fretboard in a thorough and organized fashion. The difficulty is that those same musical structures look different in different places on the fretboard, so there is a lot of memorization here. But if you're ready to put in a little repetitive practice, you can get it all burned into your brain.

The Pentatonic Boxes

The minor pentatonic shape you learned earlier is called "box 1" or the "primary box." You can, however, play the same scale (the same five tones) in other locations all over the neck. In fact, there are five different "box" shapes covering the fretboard. Below they are shown in Em. Notice that at the twelfth fret, the boxes repeat. Play up and down through all these shapes until they are memorized.

> TIP: To help learn these shapes faster, focus on one box shape below, excluding all other shapes. Use the scale memorization method explained earlier on CD track 35 until that shape is familiar to you. Then move on to the next one. Do the same for each shape until you have covered the entire fretboard.

Example 97 – **Em Pentatonic, 5 Boxes**

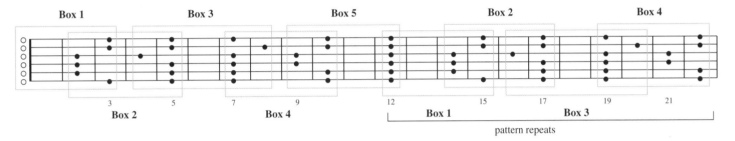

When we change keys, all the boxes shift together, as with any scale. The staff/tab examples below show a few methods of approaching this set of shapes to help memorize them even better.

> TIP: Start slow of course and build up your speed as you are comfortable.

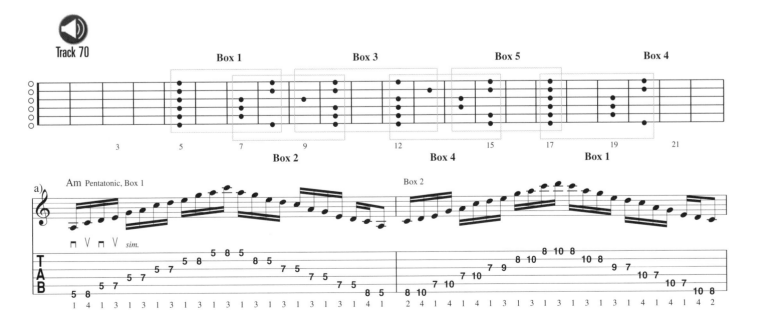

89

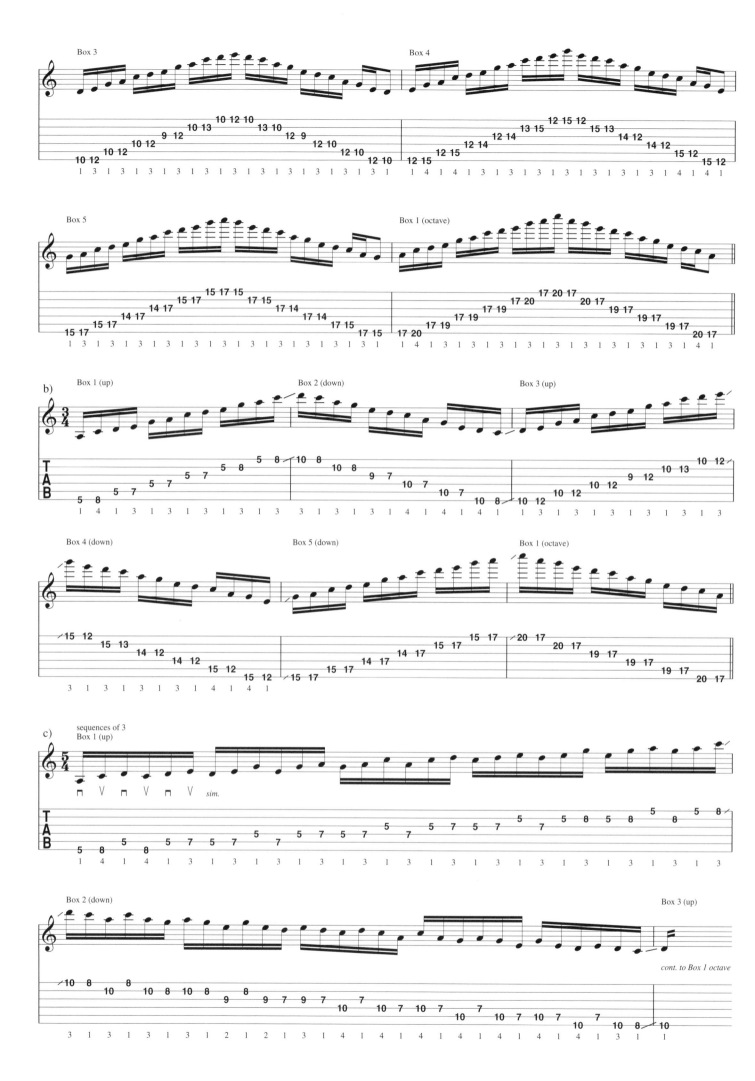

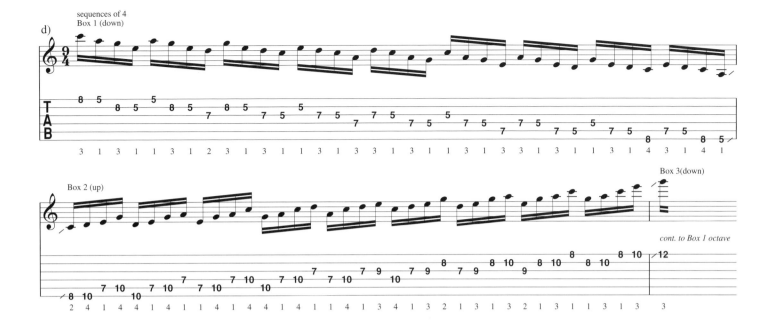

FYI: The five different scale shapes are musically identical in that they consist of the same five tones per octave. They only look different due on the guitar due to the tuning. This is the nature of a chromatic instrument like guitar. One the one hand, the parallel nature of scales is readily apparent—changing keys is as simple as sliding the entire scale/chord pattern. But the downside is that we have to learn each musical structure in five different shapes instead of one.

Here are a few diagonal shapes of the minor pentatonic that you will run into from time to time. These are based upon the primary box (1) and secondary box (4) with added lower and upper extensions, which simply shift into the next lower and higher boxes, respectively. They appear below in the key of Gm, but of course these diagonal shapes can appear in any key. Play them in E, F♯, A, B♭, C, and D as well.

Example 99 – **Gm Pentatonic, Diagonals**

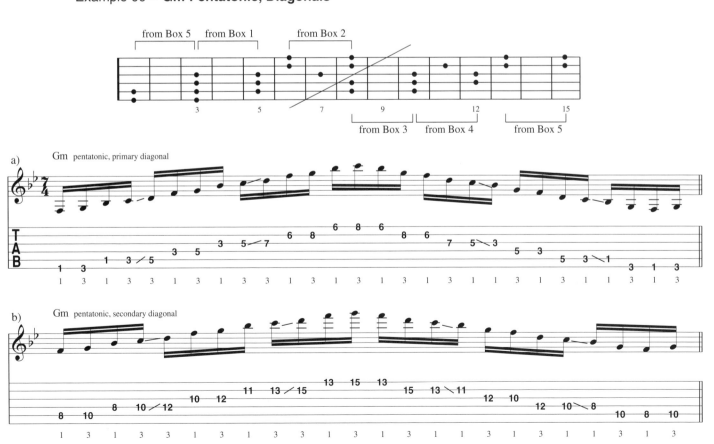

What we really want to achieve here is the ability to freely "float" all over the fretboard through these pentatonic shapes, changing at will. There's no need to stick with any particular predefined "diagonal" pattern; you want to be open to *all* possibilities. Here is an exercise to help you begin to see the patterns horizontally on the neck—so you're not stuck in the box shapes.

Example 100a – **Pentatonic Exercise #1**

Track 71

Finally, turn on your metronome or drum machine and simply improvise at a moderate tempo, shifting at random through the pentatonic patterns in the key of your choosing. Start by playing even eighth or sixteenth notes, freely drawing upon sequences or contours as you like. After this becomes comfortable, try sustaining notes or rests, repeating melodic motifs, and even using string bends.

TIP: When bending the strings, keep it in the pentatonic scale for now by always bending either a whole step (two frets) or minor 3rd (three frets) up to the next higher note in the scale. If you're not sure of the distance to the next higher note, stop and visualize the next higher box shape and you can graphically see whether it's up two or three frets.

Example 100b – **Pentatonic Exercise #2, Improv**

Improv, transcribed from recording:

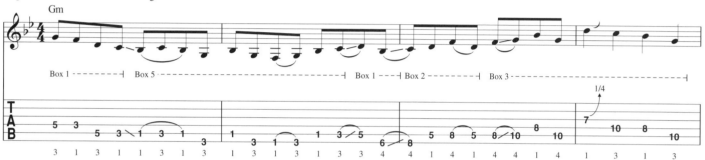

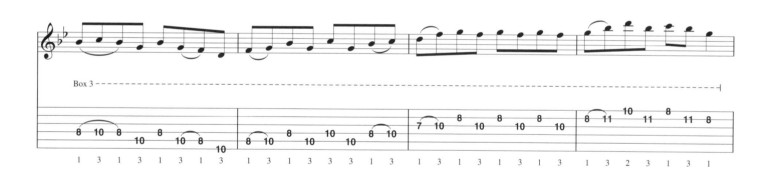

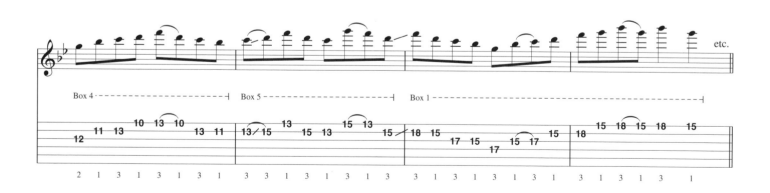

Anchors and Pentatonic Tones

When we first considered the minor pentatonic scale box 1 (back in Part II) we learned it not as a dot pattern, but as musical intervals that you recognized by sound. We must now do the same thing with the tones of boxes 2–5. Of course the job is easier now, because you already know the pentatonic tones.

First, let's break up the box "dots" by identifying the roots. These are our anchor points. Play each box slowly and refer to the diagram below, noting the position of each root. Then the tones extend up a minor 3rd to ♭3, then a whole step up to 4, a whole step up to 5, and a minor 3rd up to ♭7. Looking in the reverse direction, the ♭7 tone is always a whole step below the root.

> TIP: Yeah, this may look incomprehensible at first glimpse, but if you break it up properly it's really not so bad. Play through each box very slowly, saying the names of each tone out loud and pausing on the roots. Soon you'll begin to see similarities and parallelisms within these shapes.

Example 101 – **Am Boxes with Root Anchors, Tones Labeled**

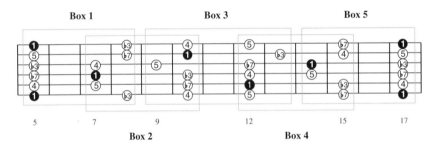

> FYI: Each pattern follows the same intervallic structure, from root to octave root:

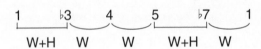

Each octave box only looks different because it lays across the strings differently, using "alternative" interval shapes and/or because it crosses between strings 2 and 3 (page 28).

The same short lick is played in each box in example 102. Play it and write out the intervallic tones relative to the root. Then play the same lick in each of the other boxes.

Example 102 – **Moving Licks Between Boxes**

Track 73

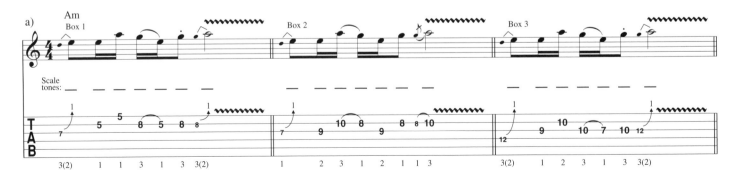

TIP: This is an excellent way to begin to use all the boxes more musically. Try moving all other pentatonic licks you already know into these other boxes. Some will fit well, and others may be rather difficult. That's okay—different boxes lend themselves to certain licks better than others.

Next we're going to superimpose full chord shapes to use as even bigger "anchors" behind the minor pentatonic boxes. There are five different barre-chord shapes on the guitar, which correspond to the five pentatonic boxes. Below are the five open chord shapes, followed by the barre-chords derived from them.

Example 103 – **Open Major Shapes and Barre Chord Derivatives**

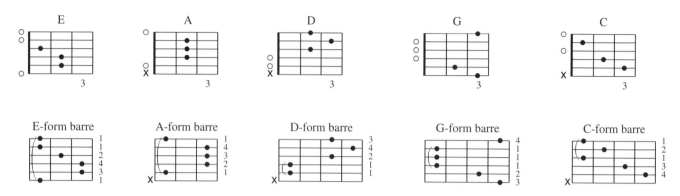

FYI: A *barre chord* is a movable chord shape that can be used to play any letter-named chord. It requires one finger to lay flat across (or "barre") two or more strings. You simply slide the shape up or down the neck to place the root of the chord on the correct note to play the major chord of the same name. Do not confuse the names of these five *shapes* ("E-form," "A-form," "D-form," "G-form," and "C-form") with the actual letter names of a specific chord. You can use any of these five forms to play *any* letter-named chord. For example, you could play an A chord using the E-form shape, A-form shape, D-form shape, G-form shape, or C-form shape.

Here are the five different forms for an E major chord. Notice how each shape links with the others. The easiest way to memorize this is by locating the two most common barre chords first—the E-form (primary) and A-form (secondary). Below, these are labeled in bold face.Then, look at the D-form as an extension from the E-form, and the G-form an extension from the A-form. C-form completes the picture by sprouting "backwards" from the root of the A-form.

Example 104 – **Five Forms of E Major Chord**

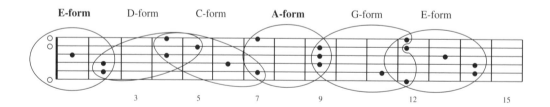

FYI: Some of these are particularly difficult to play in their full shapes. But various partial versions of each of these are very commonly used.

Now lay the pentatonic boxes against, or "superimposed over," the chord shapes. Each box is associated with a particular chord shape. Play each chord (circled notes) and then play the pentatonic scale in that location (numbered tones). If you know the voicing of the chord shapes, it will be much easier to see the tones of minor pentatonic. (The roots and 5ths help break up the patterns and lend a structure to things.)

TIP: Notice the mismatched tone below. The major chord (1–3–5) and minor pentatonic scale (1–♭3–4–5–♭7) disagree on the 3rd tone. However, this imperfect fit is intentional. First of all, it is not uncommon to use major 3rds in a minor pentatonic context in licks, and this method clearly defines the locations of all major 3rds. But even more fundamentally, it allows us to easily peg the locations of all 3rds (major or minor) in both the chord shapes and the minor pentatonic shapes, which helps us memorize all the tones on the fretboard that much faster.

Example 105 – **Em Pentatonic with Major Chord "Anchors"**

Major Pentatonics

The trick to instantly transform minor pentatonic scales (and licks) into their major counterparts is to shift the patterns down three frets, while holding the root the same. Let's walk through the procedure to locate the A major pentatonic scale shapes. Start with the Am pentatonic shapes and shift all five patterns down three frets. Now we have F♯m pentatonic. Since A major and F♯ minor are relative major and minor, the A major pentatonic and F♯ minor pentatonic scales share the same notes (but have different roots). The key point here, though, is that since they share the same notes, they share the same patterns. The final step to view these F♯m pentatonic shapes as A major pentatonic shapes is simply to view this set of shapes with the A roots and "anchor chords."

Example 106 – **F#m Pentatonic to A Major Pentatonic**

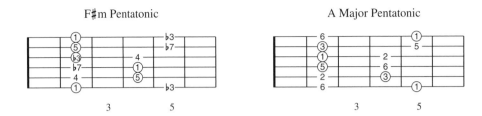

F#m Pentatonic   A Major Pentatonic

FYI: It's easy enough to transform your minor pentatonic licks into major, simply by dropping them three frets. But be aware that if you are playing in a major context, yet still viewing the shapes as "minor," you are not truly seeing things as they are. It is preferable to attach the correct roots and chord anchors, as this affects how you see the fretboard and therefore how you use the patterns. So strive to memorize the major pentatonics as scales in their own right, properly attached to their own anchors.

Example 107 – **A Major Pentatonic with Major Chord Anchors**

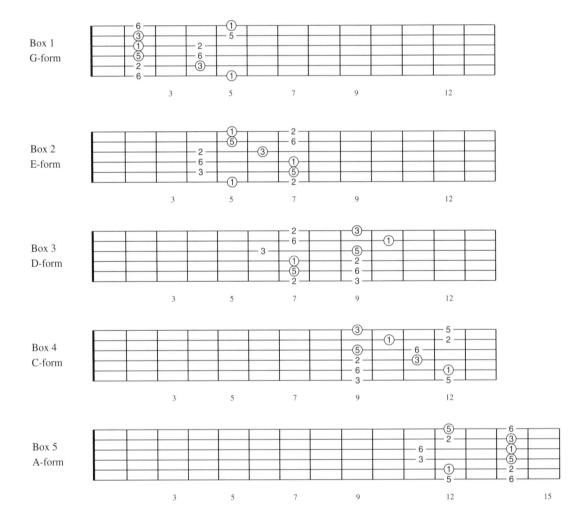

Box 1 G-form

Box 2 E-form

Box 3 D-form

Box 4 C-form

Box 5 A-form

TIP: With the chord anchors superimposed against the major pentatonic shapes, now things start looking quite different than the relative minor pentatonic. Play each chord, then play up and down through the associated pentatonic shape saying all the chord tones out loud to help memorize them.

The most common diagonals used for major pentatonic are slightly different than their minor counterparts.

Example 108 – **A Major Pentatonic, Diagonals**

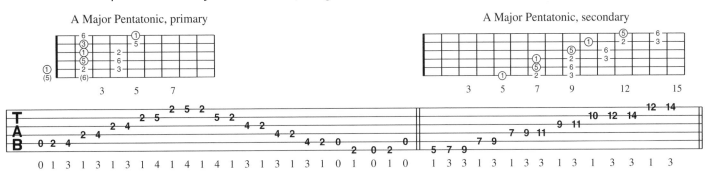

Here is a little study piece using major pentatonics. In the key of D major, the theme outlines a I–V7–IV–I progression with each chord lasting a full four measures. Over D, I'm playing D major pentatonic; over A, it's A major pentatonic mixed with A7 tones (A Mixolydian). At the IV change (G), it's actually a mini I–V–IV–V progression revolving around G. That is, the chords G–D/G–C/G are I–V–IV of IV. (Technically, the V of IV is I relative to the original key, and the IV of IV is ♭VII relative to the original key—in this case that's C. So it's not so far removed from the key of D major; still, you'll miss the function here if you don't view this little sequence as making G a temporary tonic.) At measure 21 the solo begins on A (V). Notice the use of C natural, A's parallel minor 3rd at work in measures 21 and 28. In a major context, this note gives a strong, bluesy pull. At measure 29 we drop to G (IV) and I shift to G major pentatonic in the lead. A country-blues approach that mixes minor and major is seen in measures 33–36.

Example 109 – **"Bluegrass Country-Blues Major Pentatonic Rockout"**

Track 75

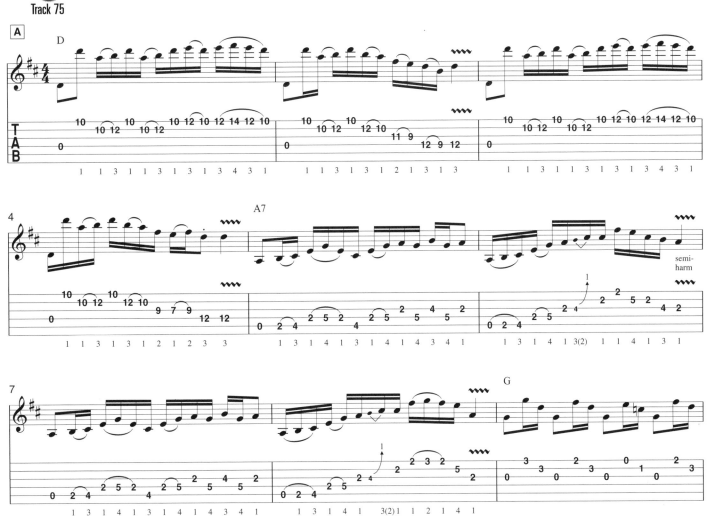

99

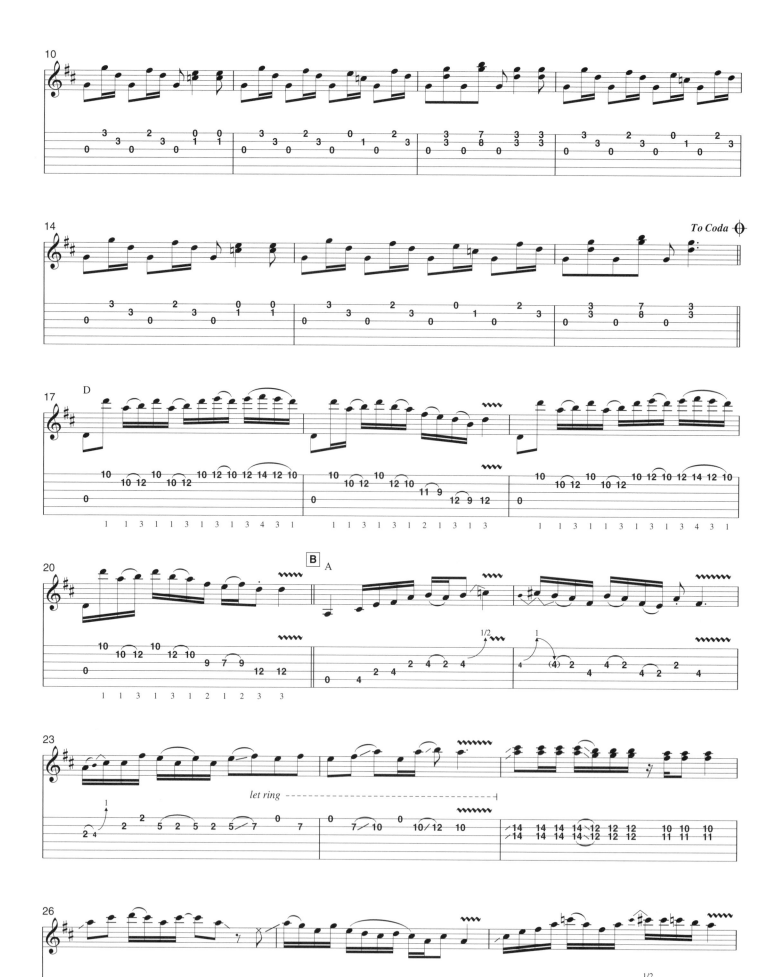

TIP: In example 109, each chord is sustained for a fairly long period. When dealing with solo situations over longer chords like this, it is common to regard each chord as its own temporary key center and change keys. That is, instead of playing D major over all three chords, I played D major pentatonic over D, A major pentatonic over A, and G major pentatonic over G. However, the prominent inclusion of G (♭7) over A is a nod toward the fact that A7 is the V chord of D. So I'm not totally ignoring the overall key here and playing in three separate keys, but almost!

FYI: A hybrid scale consisting of a major pentatonic scale with an added ♭3 tone would be the relative major counterpart of the blues scale. In other words, if you follow the same move-down-three-fret transformation method we used earlier to change from minor pentatonic to major pentatonic, but applied this to the blues scale instead of minor pentatonic, you wind up with a major pentatonic scale with an added ♭3. (The added ♭5 tone of the blues scale becomes ♭3 of the major pentatonic.) So just as you can substitute the blues scale for minor pentatonic, you can likewise substitute this major hybrid scale for straight major pentatonic. Look for this scale in the B (solo) section of example 109.

Arpeggios

If you learned the five chord shapes well, you have pretty much already learned all the major arpeggios over the fretboard. There are just a few small "cracks" left to fill. Memorize these now and fill in the correct tones in the blank spaces below. If you've done your homework up to this point, this shouldn't look too nightmarish—you should be able to see an interconnected grid work of all the familiar chord shapes. Play through the arpeggios in each area.

Example 110 – **A Major Arpeggios, Full Fretboard**

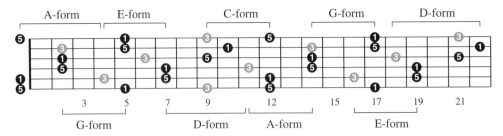

Now grab all the 3rds and yank 'em down a fret. Presto! We've got minor arpeggios! (See, this is getting easier, isn't it?) The roots and 5ths remain in the same pattern as above. Study the diagram below until the familiar minor chord shapes jump out at you. Then play through the arpeggios in each area. I'll leave the diagonals up to you.

Example 111 – **A Minor Arpeggios, Full Fretboard**

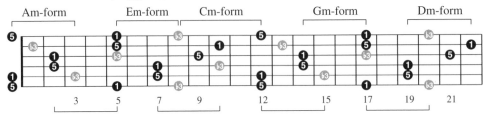

Example 112 shows the progression from the Pachelbel's Canon in D, a staple of the classical repertoire. Here we will play each chord as an arpeggio, using the same, parallel sequence for each one. Example 112a uses the top part of each primary shape (except the low D). The sample idea in 112b uses a sweep pattern. After you master these, make up some of your own by selecting different arpeggio shapes and moving them through the same progression.

Track 76

Example 112 – **Arpeggio Study ("Canon in D," J. Pachelbel)**

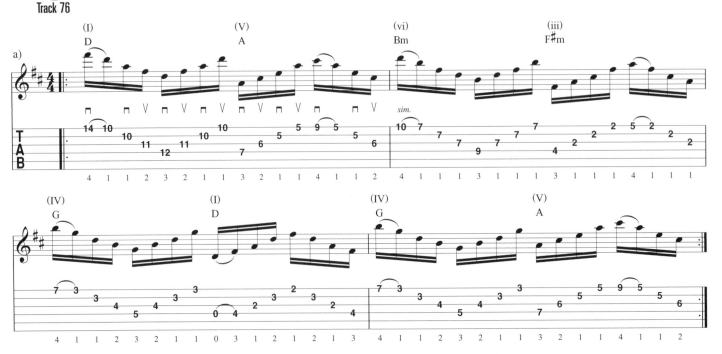

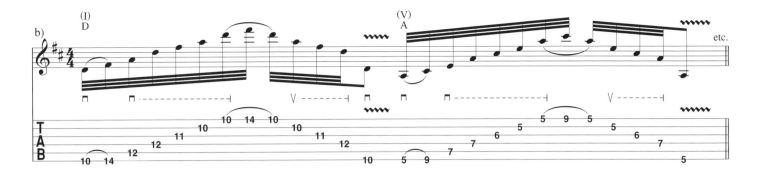

Now we are ready to add 7ths. Insert minor 7th tones (a whole step below each root) into major arpeggios and we have dominant 7th arpeggios. Insert major 7th tones (one fret below each root) and we have major 7th arpeggios. Start with minor arpeggios and add minor 7ths and we create minor 7th arpeggios. Focus on one small form at a time, playing up and down the notes in that positional shape while saying the tones out loud. So there are 27 exercises in example 113—nine in each diagram.

TIP: These diagrams are certainly getting a step more complex, and your first reaction may well be, "This is ridiculous!" If so, you are looking at too much information at once. Just patiently focus on one area at a time, to the exclusion of the others, and you will see that you already know nearly everything here. The only real difference is that we are sticking it all together, end to end.

Example 113 – **7th Arpeggios, Full Fretboard**

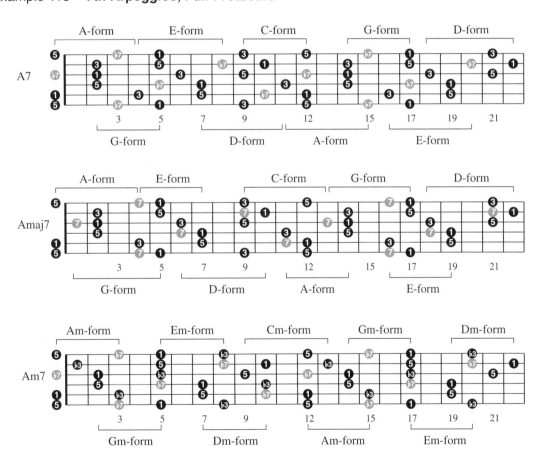

Arpeggios act as a valuable "skeletal framework" for the fretboard. They neatly divide chord tones from non-chord tones (which is the single most valuable piece of information about any individual tone). Therefore, learning these patterns is essential. In addition, you may also use arpeggios directly—slipping arpeggio-based lines into a diatonic or pentatonic context creates an interesting change.

Natural Minor Positional Patterns

We already covered the natural minor scale in its primary positional shape in Part II. Now we'll extend it over the remaining four areas of the neck, superimposed over the minor pentatonic shapes and arpeggios.

Below, the five positional areas of A natural minor are laid out. Since the A minor pentatonic scale is contained within A natural minor as a subset (and you already know it well), those box patterns are now shown in black dots with the added tones 2 and ♭6 in grey.

> Caution: These patterns build on the previous shapes. So if you don't have those pentatonic boxes and the contained arpeggio shapes memorized like the back of your hand, stop! Go back and study them until you have them fully memorized. Only then should you proceed.

Example 114 – **A Natural Minor Positional Patterns**

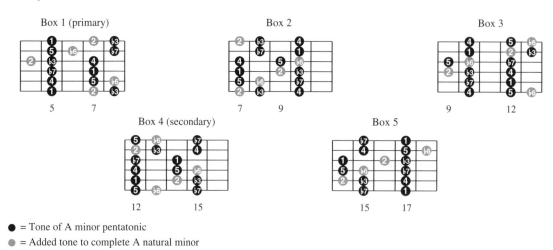

● = Tone of A minor pentatonic
● = Added tone to complete A natural minor

Below are some A natural minor licks improvised in several different areas of the fretboard. Identify the tones for each. (Answer on page 163.) Then try moving them into other keys and making up a few natural minor licks of your own.

Example 115 - **Natural Minor Positional Licks**

Track 77

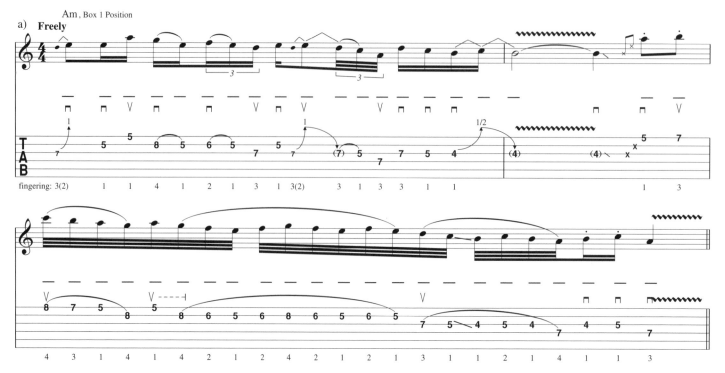

104

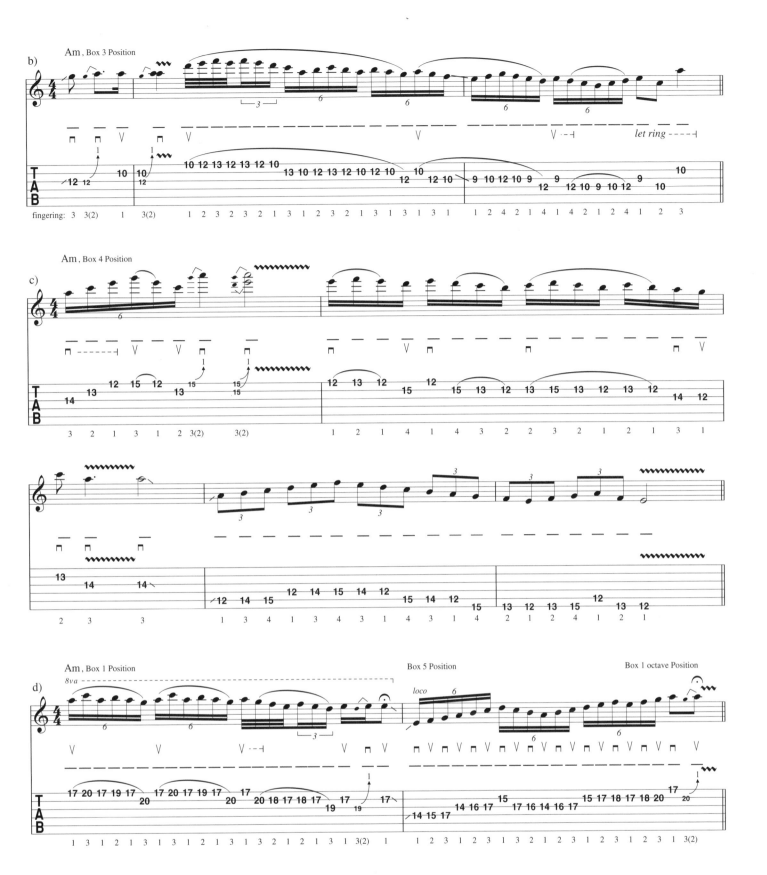

Now play the natural minor scale patterns and licks in other keys, including Em, Dm, Gm, Bm, etc.

TIP: At this point you should be able to look at the fretboard and, in any minor key, envision a framework of ever-increasing complexity, all interwoven. First, we have the roots and the chord anchor shapes. Then the arpeggios fill it out a bit more. The minor pentatonic boxes come next. And finally the diatonic minor patterns "flesh it out" the rest of the way. Knowing this "interconnectedness" within the different structures is really the answer to learning how to use scales fully.

Diatonic Major and the Modes

The major scale dot shapes are identical to those of the natural minor scale. The difference, of course, is that we must weld them to different anchor roots, chords, arpeggios, etc. So the dot pattern is the same, but the tones are all different.

CAUTION: Do not continue here until you have conquered the major pentatonic shapes! These diatonic patterns build on and contain the major pentatonic patterns.

Example 116 – **A Major Positional Patterns**

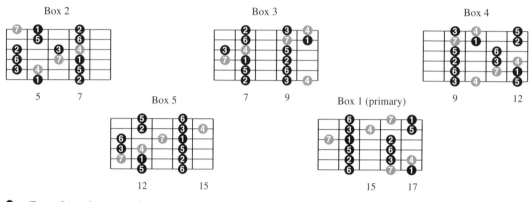

● = Tone of A major pentatonic
● = Added tone to complete A major diatonic

If you look at the shapes above—ignoring the tone numbering and differences between the black and gray dots—they should look familiar. They are the primary two-octave shape for each of the major modes that you learned back in example 49. They are also the same shapes as in the natural minor scale in example 114. Of course, it is the anchoring structure and tonal numbering that make it different. And that makes all the difference.

Now we will change the anchor structure (and tonal numbering) to transform all these patterns into each mode specifically. We will do this by superimposing the pentatonic shapes, which at this point you should have thoroughly mastered.

TIP: The minor modes (Dorian and Phrygian) will use the minor pentatonic shape within them. The major modes (Lydian and Mixolydian) will use the major pentatonic shape. The diminished mode (Locrian) will use a minor pentatonic with its 5th step flatted. Here is the plan for the patterns following:

1. Play each position's pentatonic and then diatonic pattern, noting the anchor chord shape within that position.

2. Play the chord and arpeggio in that position followed by the full scale.

3. Finally, improvise some melodies in each position, singing along with each note as you play it. Float freely between playing arpeggio-focused melodies, pentatonic melodies, and

   diatonic melodies. Your new knowledge of scale tones and superimposed patterns will

Example 117 – **Modes in Positional Patterns**

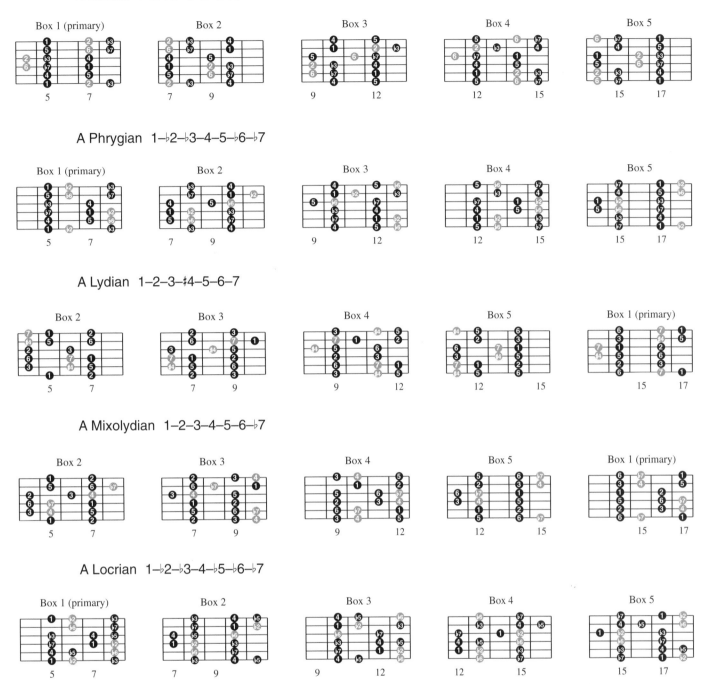

A Dorian 1–2–♭3–4–5–6–♭7

A Phrygian 1–♭2–♭3–4–5–♭6–♭7

A Lydian 1–2–3–♯4–5–6–7

A Mixolydian 1–2–3–4–5–6–♭7

A Locrian 1–♭2–♭3–4–♭5–♭6–♭7

Did you get all that?! Test yourself with the parallel scale improvisation exercise we did earlier in example 54. The only difference this time is that you are now free to roam about the entire fretboard! Try it! Write a random list of scales, turn on a click and start playing. You can move diagonally, positionally, or any other way. Just stay in each scale until you call out the next scale in your list, and try to change instantly, at whatever part of the fretboard you happen to be in at that moment.

Example 118 - **Parallel Scale Improv Exercise**

TIP: If your mind goes blank for a moment and you cannot locate the new scale shape in your current area of the fretboard, just sustain the note you are on and mentally search for the correct anchor points for the new scale. Then you can mentally picture the correct scale shape and pick right up with it. This isn't easy, but it will help you grasp the fretboard much quicker!

Natural Minor in Three-Notes-Per-String

For fast diatonic runs, three-note-per string shapes are great. And since they move somewhat diagonally across the fretboard, they give the added benefit of seeing various alternative methods of shifting between the positional patterns. Below are all the three-notes-per-string diatonic shapes shown in the key of Em. There are seven different patterns—one beginning on each of the seven different notes of the scale. They weave between and connect the various positional shapes.

> TIP: Pay close attention to how these patterns appear with respect to the E roots and E minor arpeggios. To emphasize the arpeggios, we have circled the chord/arpeggio tones below. For extra credit, make a series of large fretboard diagrams and write out these three-note-per-string shapes, writing in the tone for every note!
>
> TIP: Use the scale memorization method shown earlier in CD track 35, adding one note at a time. You can also reverse it, starting at the top note and adding one note at a time, progressing downward.

Example 119 - **Em Three-Notes-Per-String**

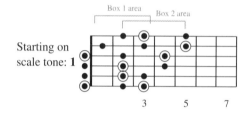

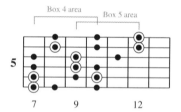

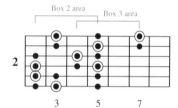

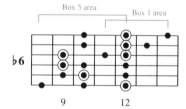

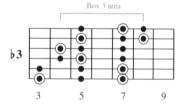

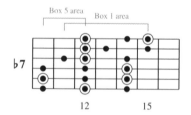

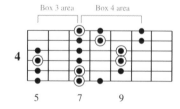

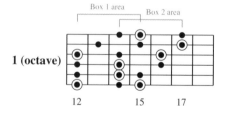

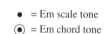

108

Here is a set of exercises to help burn these patterns into your brain. (They make great technique drills too, by the way.) First, just play up and down each shape in sextuplets, so the rhythm mirrors the scale layout itself.

Example 120 – **Em, Three-Notes-Per-String Drills**

Track 78

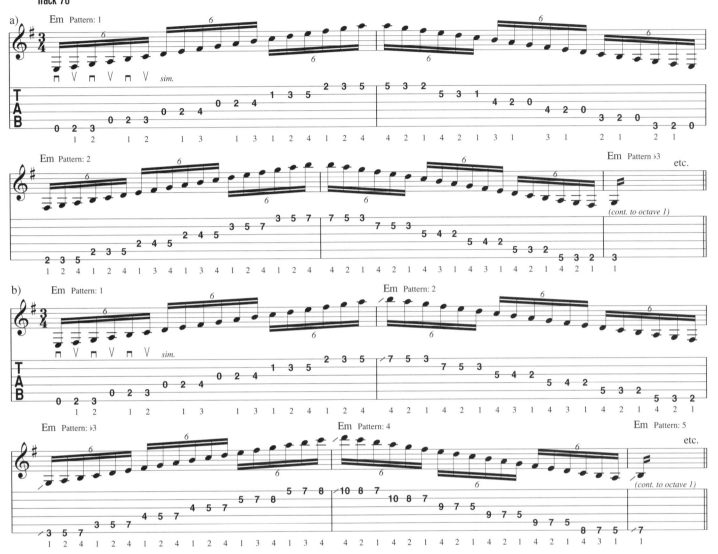

Let's move it to Am now and try some more ideas. Example 121 applies a repeating pattern to each shape.

Example 121 – **Am, Three-Notes-Per-String Drills**

Track 79

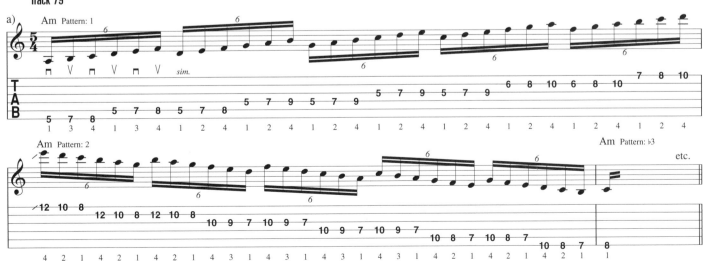

109

b)

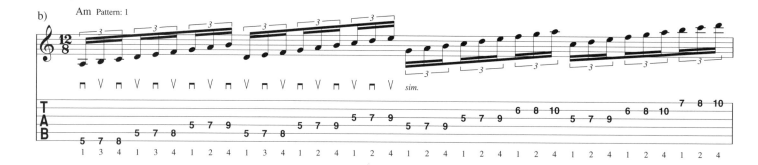

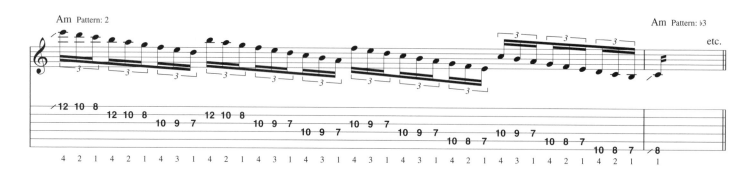

Whereas the previous example showed two "pattern derived" sequences, the following example is a "pitch-derived" sequence. That is, it is a true sequence based upon pitch, in sets of four and six. Take this on up through all remaining patterns.

Track 80

Example 122 - **Gm, Three-Notes-Per-String Sequences**

a)

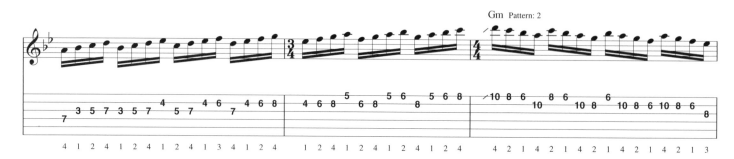

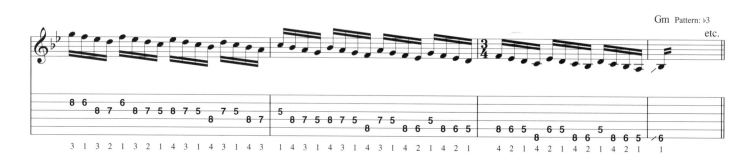

110

Now here's an extra step for the truly relentless among us. Here we break away from a steady rhythm, "cramming in" the notes to create a sense of pulse from the high note of each contour peak. So the rhythmic groupings are not particularly important—they are a consequence of the contour. Let's move the key again, this time to Fm.

Example 123 – **Fm, Three-Notes-Per-String Drills**

Track 81

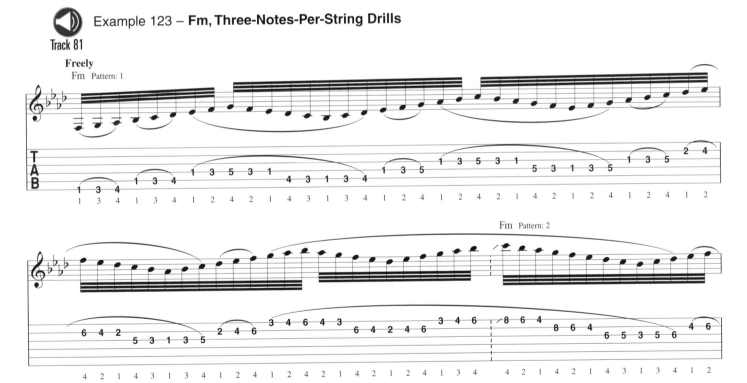

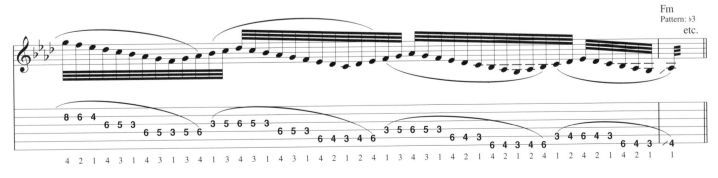

Finally, let's take the same pattern and set it against straight sixteenth notes. Since the pattern does not "line up" nicely against the rhythmic presentation, it is more interesting—and more difficult. Against a steady rhythm in sixteenth notes, the pattern plays itself out unevenly, "rolling over itself." Watch the fretboard shape to tell you when each contour should turn.

Example 124 – **Fm, Three-Notes-Per-String Drills**

Track 82

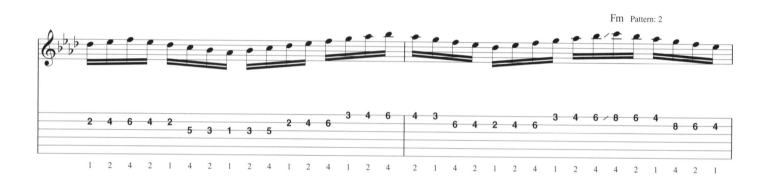

Other Scales in Three-Notes-Per-String

To transform the previous three-note-per-string shapes into major and the other modes (Dorian, Phrygian, Lydian, Mixolydian, and Locrian), it is simply a matter of changing your anchors.

G major uses the same shapes as E minor, but it's anchored to G roots, arpeggios, and major pentatonic boxes. For example 125, draw the neck diagrams for all seven shapes of G major with three-notes-per-string. (They are the same dot pattern as Em.) Then circle 1, 3, and 5. Play all the G major chords shapes within a scale pattern, then play its three-notes-per-string scale shape.

Example 125 – **Write Out G major, Three-Notes-Per-String**

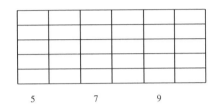

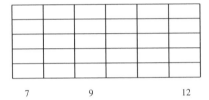

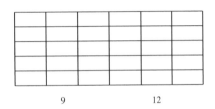

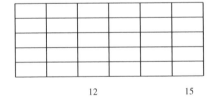

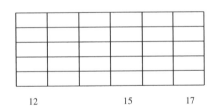

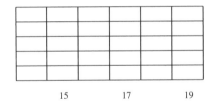

Now create or copy blank fretboard diagrams and do the same for each of the modes (Dorian, Phrygian, Lydian, Mixolydian, and Locrian), in parallel beginning on G. Then try some of the three-notes-per-string drill patterns that we used earlier on these modal shapes. (More blank fretboard diagrams can be found on page 165.)

When you've got the diatonic patterns down, harmonic minor and Phrygian-dominant are easy. Harmonic minor is natural minor with every ♭7 replaced by 7 (just one fret below each root instead of two). Phrygian-dominant is just like the standard Phrygian mode except with a raised (major) 3rd. Write these alterations out, each using seven fretboard diagrams. Then try some of the drills on these scales, and move them into a few different keys.

Example 126 – **Write out the Modes in Three-Notes-Per-String**

Example 127a – **Write Out E Harmonic Minor, Three-Notes-Per-String**

Example 127b – **Write Out E Phrygian-Dominant, Three-Notes-Per-String**

Scale "Chunking"

Scale chunking is my name for taking a large "chunk" of a scale—even a full octave—and shifting your position so that the same portion of the scale appears repeatedly. Below this idea is applied to common A major and A minor shapes.

Example 128 – **Scale Chunking in A**

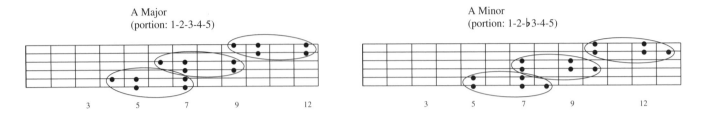

This is an excellent way to help "fill in" those mysterious areas of the fretboard that always seem so hard to remember. This method also has the advantage of easily transferring the scale tone information from one pattern into the next chunk. Used over time, this "chunking" method of seeing scales, combined with your arpeggio, pentatonic, and diatonic shapes, will make every millimeter of the fretboard feel like good, familiar territory.

> FYI: The five positional patterns can be seen as one approach to viewing scales. The extreme opposite method is laying out scales horizontally on a single string. A third method is the diagonal and three-note-per-string approach. Scale "chunking" idea qualifies as a fourth option. It's not that there is one way to view scales. All approaches offer value and are intertwined.

Below, I've omitted the 7th from the minor scale and "chunked" it over three octaves to make a fairly terrifying lick. But in fact, it's easier than it sounds when you notice the repetition operating within it.

Example 129a – **Bm Hexatonic "Chunking" Lick**

Track 83

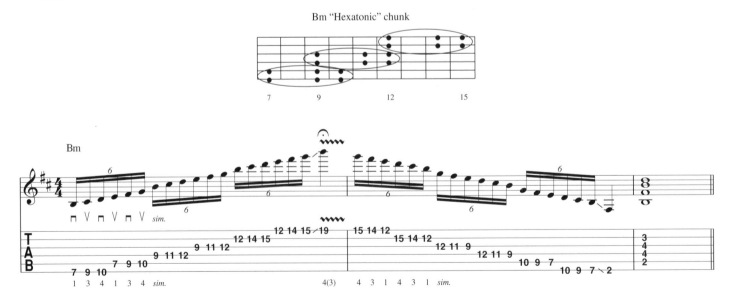

TIP: Remember to account for the extra fret when moving across strings 2 and 3.

114

Below are some diagrams to give you an idea how to apply this chuncking approach to the fretboard. At first glance they may seem complex, but notice that each circled "chunk" is identical. So it is simply repeated in other locations, like a rubber stamp! Just keep your eye on the roots to stay in the right positions.

> TIP: After you are familiar with a pattern below, invent a short sequence or run that utilizes one of the scale "chunks" and then repeat it in each pattern. This way, you can string together longer runs, which, at their heart, are really quite simple due to the repetition aspect. Also, make up a few chunking patterns of your own and make up more runs for them. You can use any scale shape or portion thereof.

> When this approach is applied enough, soon the entire fretboard will begin to fuse together along with the positional "box" shapes, the three-notes-per-string patterns, and the arpeggios. You will be able to envision numerous patterns springing in any different direction from any point on the neck. Then the fretboard really becomes your "playground."

Example 129b – "Chunking" Patterns

A Major Pentatonic

Am Pentatonic

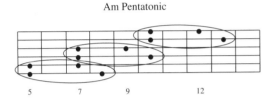

A Blues Scale

A Dorian

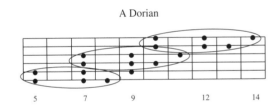

A Harmonic Minor

A Lydian

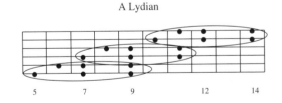

Remember, you don't always have to run straight up these patterns from low to high. Try to mix it up; build sequences within each chunk or maybe try descending through each chunk. You'll come up with some really interesting stuff this way. Next, take some licks you already know and expand them over into other portions of the fretboard using this method of scale repetition.

At this point you have enough information to fully analyze virtually any musical situation and play in any part of the neck. All you are missing is enough practice. So, seek out a few dozen songs and solos to learn. As you learn them, analyze the progression and every tone of the melody/solos. Also, get out your backing tracks and start improvising!

PART V: Advanced Concepts

Congratulations! You've made it to the last section and you already know more than 99% of all guitarists! Still, we're not finished. We have a few more advanced shapes to look at, and we'll also consider some more advanced soloing ideas.

Diminished Scales and Arpeggios

The diminished 7th chord is a diminished triad (1–♭3–♭5) with an added double-flatted 7th (♭♭7). It's unusual in that each note of the chord is an equidistant minor 3rd apart. This gives it a unique kind of "slippery" quality, as your ear cannot identify any tone as being more dominant than any other—that is, no root is immediately apparent. In fact, any of the four notes could be the root. Below is the positional shape.

Example 130a - **Diminished 7th Arpeggio, Positional**

A Diminished 7th

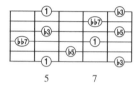

FYI: The ♭♭7 is enharmonically the same as the major 6th tone. However, in a diminished 7th chord, it functions like a 7th (the harmony a 3rd above the 5th), hence the naming.

Because the diminished 7th tones are equidistant intervals of three frets, expanding the patterns through all five areas of the neck is a breeze. Just shift up three frets and repeat, over and over.

Example 130b - **Diminished 7th Arpeggio, Extended**

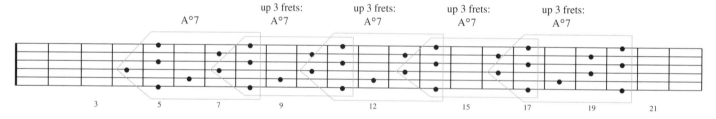

The diagonal shape is *really* diagonal. This pattern may also be moved freely up or down in three-fret increments and it remains the same arpeggio (a different inversion, but the same chord nonetheless).

Example 130c – **Diminished 7th Arpeggio, Diagonal**

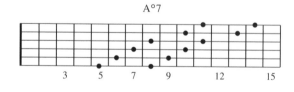
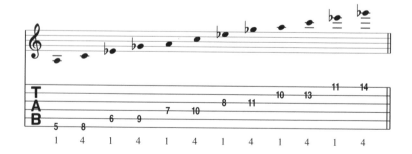

FYI: Every diminished 7th chord/arpeggio actually has four different possible names because any of the four notes could be viewed as the root. So these patterns can be A°7, C°7, E♭°7, or G♭°7 (or enharmonic equivalents). All of them are simply inversions of one another.

Harmonically speaking, there are two different ways to use diminished 7ths in modern music: you can draw on its need to resolve, or you can create a *diminished tonality*. Classically, the diminished 7th exerts a strong pull to resolve to the chord with its root one half step higher. The first lick below incorporates this classical (neoclassical) resolution. The second lick refuses to resolve and simply draws upon the tension to color the tonality very darkly. The harmonic turbulence simply "sits" there without apology.

Example 131 – **Using Diminished 7th Arpeggios in Licks**

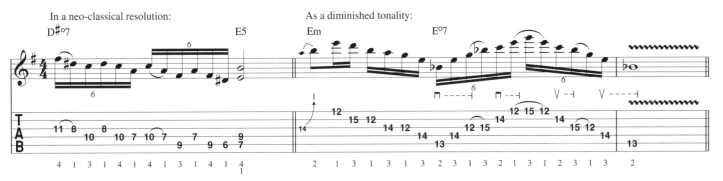

> FYI: A "diminished 7th tonality" is a bit of a contradiction in terms. The tones are equidistant and therefore none naturally presents itself as being a clear root. So it is an *atonal* structure, meaning that is has no tonal center. However, a tonal center may be imposed upon it by the use of a progression, riff, or drone.

To create a *diminished scale*, we just add a note between each chord tone of the diminished 7th arpeggio. There are two different ways to do this, which gives us two different possible diminished scales. The first begins like the natural minor scale, with a whole and then half step. This is technically known as the diminished scale, but it's commonly referred to as the *whole-half diminished scale* to distinguish it from the other form. The other option begins like the Phrygian mode, with first a half step and then whole step. This is the *half-whole diminished scale*. The patterns shown below separate the diminished 7th chord tones (in black) from the added scale tones (in grey). Note that these scales actually have eight different notes—not seven, like the diatonic modes.

Example 132 – **Diminished Scales, Positional**

> TIP: Just like the diminished 7th arpeggios, diminished scales also repeat every three frets. This makes life very easy! Practice shifting these scale patterns in three-fret increments up and down the fretboard to play the same scale in other areas of the neck.

> FYI: The diminished 7th has a double-flatted 7th tone, which is the same pitch as 6. Since that's how we've previously learned this relative pitch, that's how it is labeled above. The whole-half scale then has two 6ths. (Technically one of them is a ♭♭7, but using that label doesn't really help here—it just trades two 6ths for two 7ths.) The trouble is that we are dealing with an eight-tone, or octatonic scale, so one tone number must appear twice. The half-whole scale has two 3rds, no 4th, and two 5ths. (Technically, it has a ♭3, 4, ♭5, and ♭♭6). Octatonic scales are not a perfect fit for our diatonic scale-tone numbering system, but we can manage it. The main thing here is to separate the chord tones from non-chord tones.

Whole Tone and Chromatic Scales

The *whole tone scale* is composed entirely of whole steps (1–2–3–#4–#5–♭7). It is a *hexatonic*, or six-tone, scale. Since all tones are equidistant, it is also an atonal structure, and as with the diminished scales and arpeggios, dwelling in the whole tone scale creates a similar "slippery" or "lost" feeling. The difference here is that the color is brighter, and these tones fit nicely against the augmented chord. The lower four tones of the scale are identical to the Lydian mode.

Example 133a – **Whole Tone Scale, Positional**

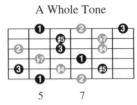

The whole tone scale may be shifted freely up and down the neck—and you will remain within the same scale—by moving the entire pattern up or down in two-fret increments (whole steps) or any multiples thereof. Here's a nice diagonal shape for the whole tone scale. This is also a perfect example of scale "chunking." Notice how the same pattern of tones repeats in the same shape three times.

Example 133b – **Whole Tone Scale, Diagonal**

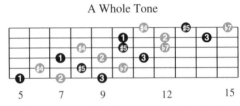

Hiding within the whole tone scale patterns is the augmented chord/arpeggio (1–3–#5). The augmented chord is also an equidistant, atonal structure, created by stacked major 3rd intervals. As you may have guessed, its shape too can be shifted freely up and down the fretboard in four-fret (major 3rd) intervals. The symbol for augmented is the plus sign (+).

Example 134 – **Augmented Arpeggios**

The chromatic scale is the ultimate atonal scale—it includes every pitch. It is rarely used in large sections. (A chromatic tonality?) Generally we see it in small doses, creating moments of passing interest, or "tonal grease," within a more standard tonality. Nevertheless, for the curious, here is the chromatic scale in a full, two-octave positional shape. Because it contains all pitches, there is only one chromatic scale. You can move this shape freely up or down the neck by any number of frets and it's still the same chromatic scale. All is one!

Example 135 – **Chromatic Scale**

Hybrid Scales

Hybrid scales are combinations of the tones from two different scales. This is just a fancy way of saying that scales are moldable and may be freely combined as you wish. Here are some hybrid scales that are worth memorizing as scales in their own right. They are sometimes called the *blues major* and *blues minor* scales.

> TIP: The black dots below are the blues scale. Added tones from the second scale are shown in grey to help you see deeper into the nature of these scales. Note the long chromatic sequences, particularly in blues-major. One might get the impression that blues players can play just about any note! Sounds about right.

Example 136 – **Blues-Major and Blues-Minor Hybrids**

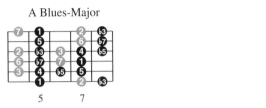

The blues-Dorian hybrid is a common rock soloing scale. And on a similar note, one of my personal favorites is a blues-diminished 7th hybrid. It's nearly the same as blues-Dorian. The difference is more a matter of how it is perceived—look for the diminished 7th arppeggio in there and draw it out.

Example 137 – **Blues-Dorian and Blues-Diminished 7th Hybrids**

Now try your hand at creating the primary positional hybrid scale shapes for A blues-natural minor, A Dorian-Mixolydian, and A major-minor. Draw in the correct dot pattern or tonal numbers on the diagrams below. Answers are on page 163.

Example 138 – **Create Hybrid Scales**

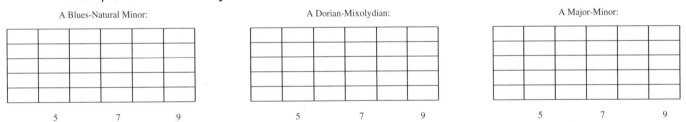

> FYI: If we can freely combine any scales to create new scales, theoretically, the number of possible scales is nearly limitless. Yet, remember what scales are—sets of tones *used in music*. So only the useful sets become canonized as *scales*. That certainly narrows it down a bit. But then again, who defines what is useful? You do! So we come full circle, back to the fact that you can make up any set of tones you like and call it a scale. Remember this rule: if it sounds good, it is good. And rule #2: there is only rule #1.

Eventually, all scales can be seen to boil down to their component tones. And when you begin to play *them*, you're not so much playing scales at all. You are choosing whatever tones you feel fit the music you want to make. So you begin to transcend scales altogether. Hybrid scales are the beginning of the end, so to speak. They show us the "crack in the armor"—and the ultimate limitation of the concept of "scale" itself.

Modes of Jazz Melodic Minor

The modes of jazz melodic minor are primarily of interest to crazy jazz and fusion players. We'll touch on them briefly, showing each in just its primary positional shape so you can get at least a passing familiarity. Below are the modes of the A jazz melodic minor parent scale.

Example 139 – **Modes of Jazz Melodic Minor**

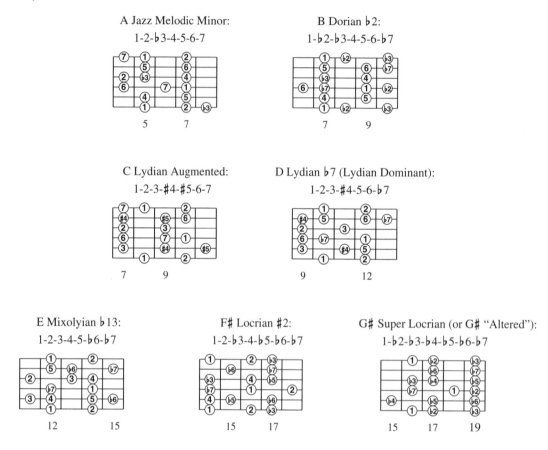

TIP: If you happen to be one of those jazz-fusion players, feel free to map out the full fretboard patterns with appropriate anchor chords for each of these scale types. If not, you've done more than enough already. But at least you can stay in the conversation when someone starts talking about Lydian ♭7 or the Altered scale. (Gee, that's *really* important.)

Extended Chord Voicing

Extended chords are those with tones above an octave, including 9ths, 11ths, and 13ths. The voicings for some common extended moveable shapes are shown below. Of course, to play any specific letter-named chord, you slide the root of the moveable shape up or down to that root note.

The 9th chords are 7ths with yet another 3rd interval stacked on top. Here are three types of 9ths with arpeggios. The standard 9th chord uses tones 1–3–5–♭7–9 (a dominant 7th with added 9th tone). The minor 9th uses tones 1–♭3–5–♭7–9 (a minor 7th with added 9th tone). The major 9th uses tones 1–3–5–7–9 (a major 7th with added 9th tone).

> TIP: We have a choice when playing arpeggios of these extended chords: do we include the upper octave roots and 3rds? If we skip them, we hear the arpeggio in a "truer" sense, meaning that the stacking up of 3rd intervals is most clearly heard. If we include them, it starts to sound more like a scale in the upper octave. Below some upper roots and 3rds are included and some are not. Notice the difference in the quality of the arpeggio that this produces.

Example 140 – **9th Chords and Arpeggios**

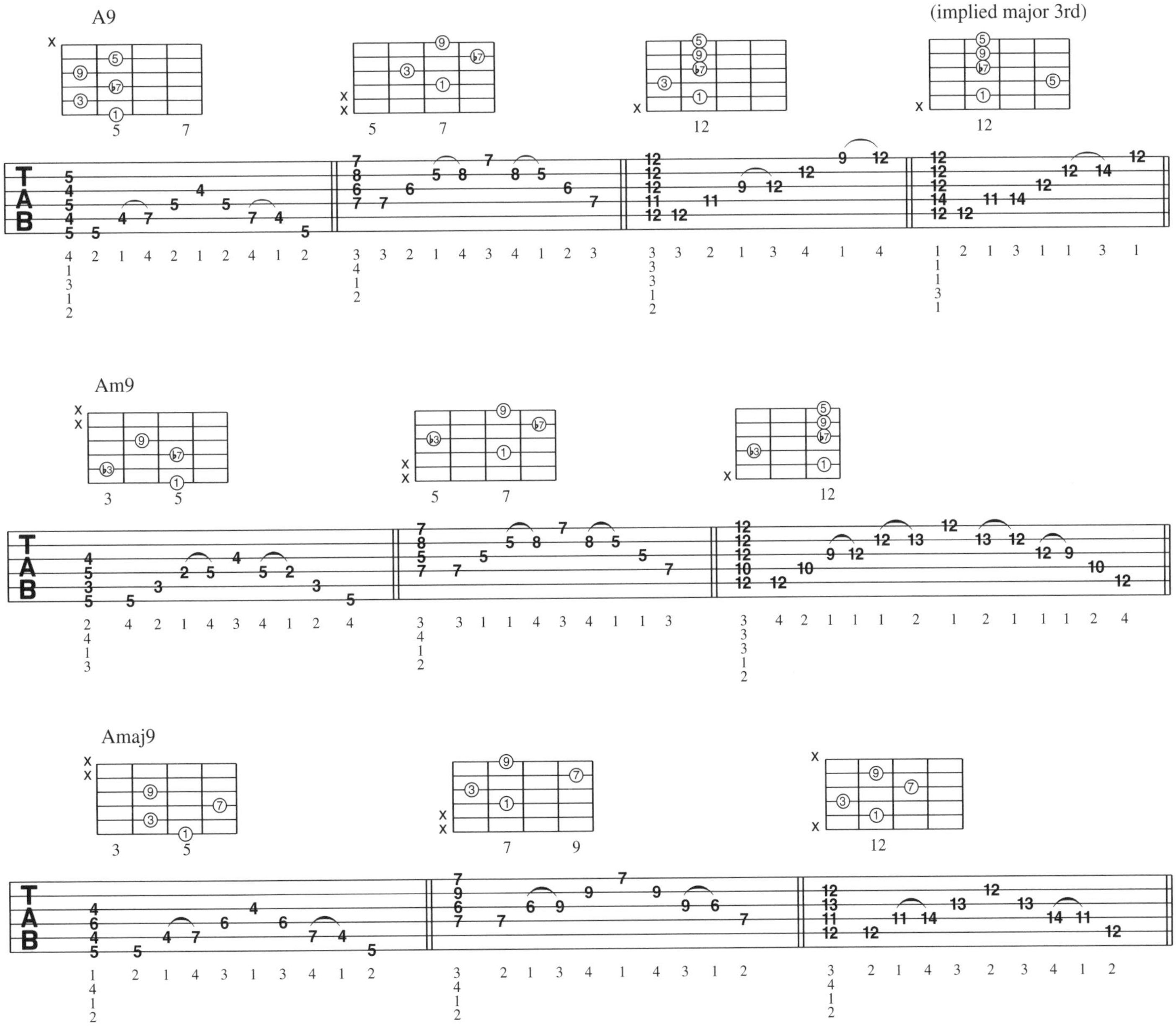

Closely related to the 9th chord is the add9 and the sus2. The difference between a 9th chord and an add9 chord is that add9 has no 7th. The sus2 chord doesn't have a 7th or a 3rd.

Example 141 – Add9 and Sus2 Chords and Arpeggios

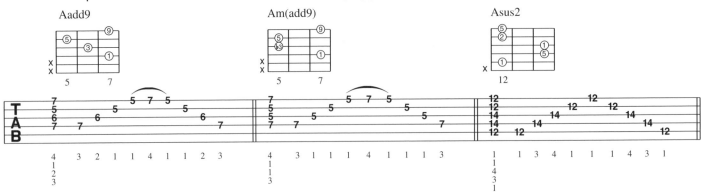

> TIP: Add9 and sus2 are nearly interchangeable, as the 2nd and 9th refer to the same tone. (Usually the 2nd of a sus2 chord is also in the higher octave just like add9.) The difference is that the add9 includes the 3rd (1–3–5–9), while a sus2 replaces the 3rd with a 2nd (1–2–5). We can infer that the name "sus2" is used because the 2nd better identifies its function as replacing the 3rd.

If we continue stacking 3rd intervals upon the 9ths, we create 11th chords. The 11th tone is an octave plus a 4th. A close relative of the 11th chord is the 9sus4. In this case we have a 4th (11th) replacing the 3rd.

Finally, if we add yet another 3rd harmony on top of an 11th chord, we get a 13th beast of a chord and we've gone all the way. (The 13th tone is the same as the 6th. Add another 3rd on top of that and you wind up back at the root.) The 13th chord contains every tone within a diatonic scale: 1–3–5–7–9(2)–11(4)–13(6). Only by separating the upper octave tones do we avoid sounding a noisy "tone cluster."

> TIP: Just as with 9th chords, there are many varieties of 11th and 13th chords, including dominant (11th and 13th), major (maj11 and maj13), and minor (min11 and min13), as well as variants. The 11th tone is commonly omitted from 13th chords with major 3rds (which includes the major and dominant variety) because it clashes with the 3rd of the chord. (Remember, the 11th is the same as the 4th tone, just an octave higher.) When the 11th is included, it is often raised a half step to create a 13♯11 chord. In minor 13th chords, the 11th is usually left unaltered because it does not clash with the ♭3rd.

These are large chords, with a lot of notes, so we can't always play all their notes on the guitar—some tones must be omitted and their presence implied. In general, the "color" tones are usually included—such as 3rds, 7ths, and the highest extension of the chord (depending on if it's a 9th, 11th, or 13th chord)—while the 5th and even the root sometimes may be omitted. For example, if we had an A13 chord, we may voice it from bottom to top: A–G–C♯–F♯ (1–♭7–3–13). Even though there are several omissions here (the 5th, 9th, and 11th), the 13th sound is still clear because the important color tones (in this case, the 3rd, 7th, and 13th) are present.

Example 142 - 11th and 13th Chords

A11 (A9sus4)

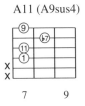

A13

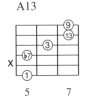

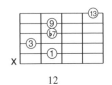

Here are some extended chord arpeggios that use sweeping/tapping and sweeping/tapping/sliding techniques. Listen for their unusual sound as they hit the upper-octave extensions and then return back to "solid ground." Play them fast enough and you'll see why I call them "insane arpeggios." They have a bit of a jazzy flavor, but they're quite at home in rock or metal soloing, as well as progressive or fusion—any style where lead technique will be appreciated and the guitarist can take the spotlight for a moment.

TIP: On CD track 84 these arpeggios are played moderately fast, so you can get a sense of them yet still hear the notes individually. Speed them up even more and the tonality of these pitch sets begins to "fuse together" even more, making them that much more bizarre and terrifying! These sweeps are very difficult to play fast, though. Here are some practice tips: 1) Break them apart into bite size pieces; practice each piece repeatedly to build up your speed, then string them back together. 2) Don't overplay. If certain notes are getting botched here and there, slow down. Don't sacrifice clarity for speed, or you'll never get these to sound smooth and clear. 3) You may prefer to tap with your middle finger so that you can continue to hold the pick between thumb and index. This makes it easier to switch quickly between picking and tapping.

 Example 143 – **Insane Arpeggios**

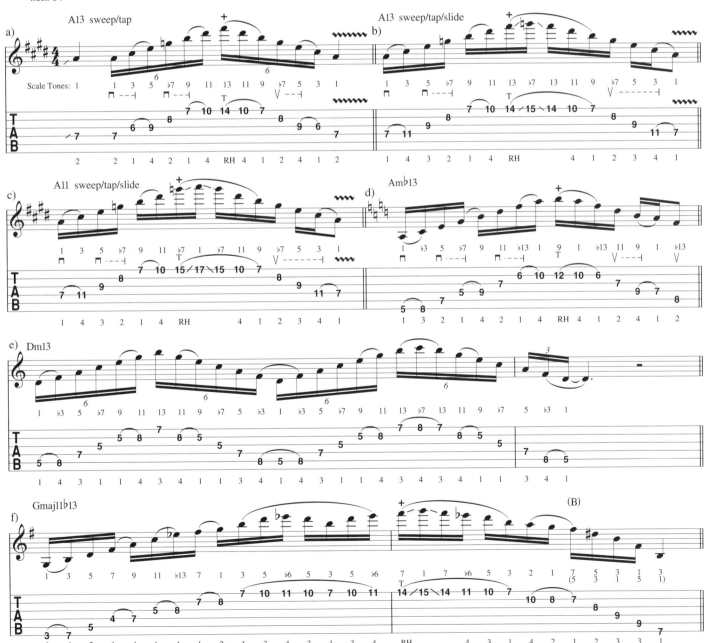

Now make up a few extended sweep/tapping licks of your own to toss into an unsuspecting solo. Or better still, make up a sequence of four or five of these in a progression and leave your listeners in the dust! (For more practice with sweep picking arpeggios in regard to technique, check out *Speed Mechanics for Lead Guitar*, Part II.)

Altered chords are extended chords in which the 5th or one of the extensions has been sharped or flatted. Why are only these tones alterable? Well, because if you alter the other notes (the root, 3rd, or 7th), you change the entire foundation of the chord. Here are a few altered chord types. Play each and check out the voicing. Then see if you can develop a few crazy arpeggios based on some of these.

Example 144 – **Altered Chord Voicings**

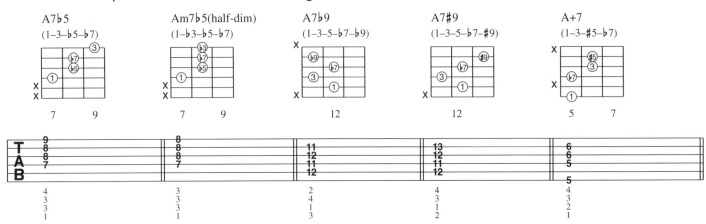

FYI: We have only looked at these chords each in just one possible shape. If you want to explore advanced chords in more detail and use them in some progressions, check out my pocket guide book, *Barre Chords: The Ultimate Reference Guide*.

Fretboard Mapping

Using the diagram below, map out tones over the entire fretboard. From the given root below, find and write in every possible tone in each area. Answers on page 163.

Example 145 – **Fretboard Mapping Exercise**

Root = A

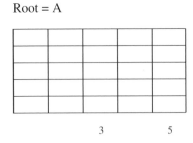

Root = C

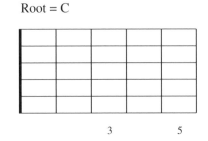

Root = E

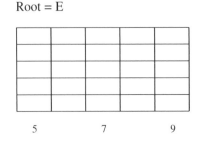

Altered Tunings

Everything in this book thus far has been in standard tuning. But don't fear, all of this applies to other tunings as well. First, let's look at the easy ones. *Slack tuning* means you tune all strings down evenly across the board. For example, E♭ slack tuning (down a half step) or D tuning (down a whole step) are common slack tunings. So the absolute pitch of all notes will sound lower, but all the tonal relationships and shapes remain intact. In fact, the common practice is that we continue to regard a low E string as an "E" even though its absolute pitch may sound as E♭, D, or even lower. This in fact demonstrates the effectiveness of our relative pitch approach—as long as everything is moved together, everything sounds about the same. (Of course if you are using a chromatic tuner or communicating with another musician who is *not* in the same slack tuning as you—a keyboardist for example—you are going to have to consider the absolute pitch of your notes.)

Things change a bit when *altered tunings* are used. The most common altered tuning variant is *drop D* tuning in which the low E string is dropped a whole step to D, while all other strings remain in standard tuning. To apply the tones, intervals, and chord/arpeggio shapes to drop D tuning, we must compensate for this pitch change by raising all notes a whole step (two frets) on the low sixth string. In drop D, all letter-named notes on the sixth string must be raised two frets as well.

Example 146 – **Drop D Tuning, note and shape alterations**

Standard tuning—Low sixth string

Drop D tuning—Low sixth string

Drop-D Intervals
Power chord (5)

4th   Major 3rd   Major 6th

Drop D, D minor pentatonic   Drop D, D major

FYI: Drop D down a half step is a combination of regular drop D and a half-step slack tuning. In a tuning like this, we regard the fretboard as if it were in regular drop D and simply acknowledge the slack tuning aspect, which means that all the strings sound a half step lower across the board.

If you have built a strong enough mental picture of musical structure, these changes will be fairly easy. You simply see an altered tuning "equivalent" of standard tuning with its quick position shift on the string(s) in question. The easiest way to get this down is to write out and run through a number of scale patterns in the new tuning. Before long, you will learn to "translate" between tunings effortlessly.

TIP: Try these altered tunings and write out some common chord voicings and scale patterns, altering the shapes as needed to compensate for the tuning changes. (In some of the extreme cases, scales become virtually impossible to play across certain strings. Just skip over that and look for important chord intervals like 5ths and octaves in those cases.)

Double drop D:	D–A–D–G–B–D
Open D:	D–A–D–F♯–A–D
Open G:	D–G–D–G–B–D
Drop B:	B–A–D–G–B–D
Drop A:	A–A–D–G–B–D

Exotic and Ethnic Scales

For the curious, here are a few oddities to check out. Who knows? One of these may inspire a monstrous song in you. Instead of giving you fretboard shapes, though, I will simply describe the tonal structure—because at this point that's all you should need. Just play one octave of each scale in the primary position (such as beginning on A at the 5th fret). The easiest way to do this is to pick a scale you already know that is fairly close, with some tones in common, and then simply alter the tones as needed "on the fly." To take it further you can always map out full positional shapes and even the rest of the fretboard if you like.

TIP: In dissecting these scales it can be helpful to cut the scale into two halves. The lower portion that includes tones 1–2–3–4 is called the *lower tetrachord*. The upper portion that includes 5–6–7 and the octave root (8) is called the *upper tetrachord*.

The *double harmonic* scale's upper tetra-chord is the same as harmonic minor, with its characteristic minor-3rd-flanked-by-half steps at 5–♭6–7–8. But double harmonic also puts another such structure in the lower tetra-chord (the same as Phrygian-dominant at 1–♭2–3–4). Double harmonic is also known as the *Gypsy* or *Byzantine* scale.

Double harmonic: 1–♭2–3–4–5–♭6–7

The *harmonic major* scale has the same upper tetrachord of harmonic minor, but the lower portion of the standard major scale.

Harmonic major: 1–2–3–4–5–♭6–7

Hungarian gypsy minor is a natural minor scale with a raised 4th. This creates the characteristic "harmonic structure" of a minor 3rd-flanked-by-half steps at 2–♭3–♯4–5. It also gives us a chromatic sequence at ♯4–5–♭6.

Hungarian gypsy minor: 1–2–♭3–♯4–5–♭6–♭7

The straight *Hungarian minor* scale is a harmonic minor scale with a raised 4th. This creates a scale with two structures of the minor 3rd-flanked-by-half steps. (Unlike double harmonic, though, the lower structure appears between tones 2–5.) *Hungarian major* has a ♯2 (same as ♭3) and a major 3rd. A bit strange.

Hungarian minor: 1–2–♭3–♯4–5–♭6–7
Hungarian major: 1–♯2–3–♯4–5–6–♭7

The *enigmatic scale* is as odd as its name implies. It begins like Phrygian-dominant, then turns into a whole tone scale, and finally turns chromatic as it leads toward the upper root. That's just freaky.

Enigmatic: 1–♭2–3–♯4–♯5–♯6–7

Don't know who the Neapolitans were, but I like their ice cream better than their scales. *Neapolitan major* does *not* have a major 3rd. Presumably, the upper portion of the scale was major was enough for them. You can think of Neapolitan major as a melodic minor scale with a ♭2nd. *Neapolitan minor* shares the same lower tetrachord as Neapolitan major, but the upper portion is that of natural minor. Another name for Neapolitan minor, as you may have noticed, is the Phrygian mode.

Neapolitan major: 1–♭2–♭3–4–5–6–7
Neapolitan minor: 1–♭2–♭3–4–5–♭6–♭7

The *bebop* or "bop" scales came into use in the jazz bebop era. The first is a Mixolydian mode with an added major 7th tone in between the ♭7th and the root. The second is a Mixolydian mode with an added ♭3rd. These are all *octatonic*, or "eight tone" scales.

Bebop dominant: 1–2–3–4–5–6–♭7–7
Bebop minor: 1–2–♭3–3–4–5–6–♭7
Bebop half-diminished: 1–♭2–♭3–4–♭5–5–♭6–7

Here are a few more oddities to consider. *Major Locrian* has the upper tones of Locrian but turns the 2nd and 3rd steps both major. *Lydian minor* has the lower tones of Lydian but turns the upper portion of the scale to natural minor. The *overtone* scale is another name for the Lydian dominant scale, which is the 4th mode of melodic minor. The *leading whole tone* scale is a standard whole tone scale with an added major 7th, creating a three-note chromatic sequence leading to the octave root. The *augmented* scale is truly bizarre sounding. It's another symmetrical scale that alternates minor 3rds with half steps.

Major Locrian: 1–2–3–4–♭5–♭6–♭7
Lydian minor: 1–2–3–♯4–5–♭6–♭7
Overtone (Lydian dominant): 1–2–3–♯4–5–6–♭7
Leading Whole Tone: 1–2–3–♯4–♯5–♯6–7
Augmented: 1–♯2–3–5–♭6–7

The scale we generally associate with the "middle-Eastern sound" is Phrygian-dominant. This scale also goes by the name *Spanish, Flamenco, Spanish-flamenco, Jewish,* and *Phrygian major.* It is used widely in ethnic styles throughout the Mediterranean, Balkans, mid-East, and north Africa. This of course is no accident—it spread through these areas with the rise of the Moorish and Mohammedan empires during the Middle Ages. But of course, this isn't the only scale used in these regions. Consider these as well:

Arabian: 1–2–3–4–♭5–♭6–♭7 (same as Major Locrian)
Egyptian: 1–2–4–5-♭7 (third "mode" of minor pentatonic)
Algerian: 1–2–♭3–♯4–5–♭6–7
Persian: 1–♭2–3–4–♭5–♭6–7
Mohammedan: 1–2–♭3–4–5–♭6–7 (same as harmonic minor)
Byzantine: 1–♭2–3–4–5–♭6–7 (same as double harmonic)

> FYI: There is more to creating the specific sound of an ethnic musical style than simply utilizing its tone set. The instrumentation used, as well as the way those tones are used melodically, plus the entire rhythmic and harmonic approach, must be factored in to create the total sonic picture.

The *Hindu* scale is the same as Mixolydian with a ♭13, or the 5th mode of melodic minor. However, traditional Indian music is actually based on the *semitone scale*, which consists of the twelve chromatic pitches of Western music plus those that lie in between!

Hindu: 1–2–3–4–5–♭6–♭7

Oriental music is most often based on pentatonic scales. The *Chinese* scale is not only defined by its five tones but also its unique method of harmonization. (The tones to the right of the slash in the Chinese formula are the harmony notes.)

Japanese: 1–♭2–4–5–♭6
Hirajoshi: 1–2–♭3–5–♭6
Chinese: 1/4–3/5–♯4/6–5/8–7/9 (harmony appears to the right of slash)
Mongolian: 1–2–3–5–6 (same as major pentatonic)
Oriental: 1–♭2–3–4–♭5–6–♭7

Here are a few more unusual pentatonics—the *Pelog, Kumoi, Iwato,* and *Balinese* scales.

Pelog: 1–♭2–♭3–5–♭6
Kumoi: 1–♭2–4–5–♭6 (same as Japanese)
Iwato: 1–♭2–4–♭5–♭7
Balinese: 1–♭2–♭3–5–♭6

All these bizarre scales can become overwhelming, to the point that one may rightly ask, "Just how many scales do I really need?" Thankfully, not all of them. The scales you need to actually memorize are a function of your musical goals and the stylistic range in which you want to achieve facility.

Yet even for the most ambitious scale-hunter, at some point the issue of scales falls by the wayside. You ultimately progress to the point where you know the intimate qualities and subtle tendencies of each scale tone, as well as the various scale settings in which each tone can appear. When you reach this stage, you have really gone beyond scales. Scales are, after all, just the sum of all the individual tones that make them up. So when you know the building blocks well, you are free to simply create your own scales as needed.

In fact, eventually you reach the point where you may be aware of the various scale patterns under your fingers, but you do not play from them or "out" of them. You play out of a sense of melody in your own mind. The patterns that form themselves under your fingers are a byproduct of the process—not the cause. When this happens, you have transcended scales!

Soloing Over Riffs & Progressions

"How does one solo over chord progressions?" Over the years, this is the most common question I have been asked by guitarists. It's also difficult to answer because there isn't just one way to do it. It's a stylistic issue. The correct answer to a jazz player will be somewhat different than it will be to a blues, rock, or metal player. It's also a matter of personal choice. What kind of melody or solo quality are you trying to create? Different approaches yield different qualities of outcome. But at its core it basically comes down to creating melodies over progressions. Soloing just tends to be a bit faster with more complex embellishments—or sometimes even entire "subroutines" within the larger melodic motions. So yes, it is possible to answer this question, and I will attempt to do this by starting with the simplest guidelines and progressing to the most advanced.

1. The first "rule" for how to play over chord progressions is simply to *find the key of the progression and play within it*. (Of course if the progression borrows from another key temporarily, you will need to accomodate this in your solo.)

2. You can always omit tones. No law says you must play every available tone. So to solo over a natural minor progression, an easy choice would be minor pentatonic. You can also freely add tones. Chromatics are of no consequence harmonically. So for example, in any situation where the minor pentatonic works, the blues scale (added ♭5) will also work. And you can add any other passing tones. But keep in mind that *adding* tones to a scale isn't the same as *substituting* tones. Playing a ♭6 when the key calls for 6 will probably sound like a wrong note (unless you are using both ♭6 and 6 together). So what we are really saying here is that you can freely augment the key but not clash against it.

3. If a progression is harmonically sparse, you are free to "fill it out" and complete it as you wish. For scale steps not specified in the underlying progression or riff, you are probably free to use any variant of these tones (or not use them at all). So over a simple A5–G5 progression, which consists of the tones A, E (A5), G, and D (G5), potential scales could include A minor pentatonic, A blues, A natural minor, A Dorian, A Phrygian, A Phrygian dominant, A Mixolydian, etc. (But melodic minor or harmonic minor wouldn't be a wise choice, because the G♯ in those scales would clash with the G5 chord.) Let your ear determine the best fit.

4. Finally, even "wrong" notes will work if you use them skillfully. In a situation where the key suggests a major 6th tone, suppose you used the minor 6th (a no-no). Even this could work, however, if you used it as an upper-neighbor tone—to embellish a fall back to the 5th—or an altered approach tone, pulling into the major 6th. There's actually a fairly easy way to accomplish this "on the fly." If a note sounds sour, just bend it up immediately until it sounds good, and then continue on as if nothing happened! Ultimately then, you can play any note you like, as long as you make it work!

So the only "rule" that encompasses all this: *As long as the notes you choose do not specifically clash against the backing chords, you're okay. And if they do clash, you're okay if you resolve it reasonably quickly or with some sort of purpose.*

However, what about the blues? It is largely based on the premise of an implied major backing key with clashing minor tones (usually ♭3 and ♭7) played over it in the lead. These are the so-called "blue" notes that gave this style its name. So some clashes are fine, even desirable. We must revise our clashing rule then, to this: *don't clash against the backing chords unless you like the clash and it sounds good.*

It seems as though we're coming full circle back to "no rules." And that's about right. It's all about wisely deciding which rules to break and in what context. So my best advice is simply to engrain all the knowledge in this book and then follow your own inner ear.

Now let's talk about the issue of following the underlying chords in a progression. Again, there are no "rules" here, only choices that will produce different results:

1. You can follow the chord progression somewhat and play off the tension/release of their chord tones to create a more melodic sound.

2. You can ignore the underlying chords of the progression and play straight licks based on the tonic. This may create a subtle "melodic suspension" between the solo and the underlying chords at times, which is resolved when the progression moves back to the tonic.

3. You can extend the harmonies of the chords in the progression if you like. Simply add a 7th or 9th tone to straight triads, for example. The most extreme application of this principle can be seen in the pitch axis technique of example 92. Here the harmony of the backing chord is simply the keynote (1) and the lead guitar manufactures scales, modes, and arpeggios at will. Between these two extremes, there is a whole spectrum of options.

4. Always be on the lookout for parallel tonality and key changes in the underlying progression. You have to change with these. You can also insert parallel tonality changes if you are on your toes by noting chords within the progression that are ambiguous and lend themselves to being extended into a parallel tonality.

TIP: Don't forget about the "quick and dirty" method of playing over progressions: just play licks drawn generally from the overall key (without any specific regard to underlying chords of the progression) and then simply follow your ear to favor a passing tone here or there, lending a hint of "melodicism" to things. This approach splits the difference between 1 and 2 above and is fairly easy to implement. It's your best bet for improvising.

Outside Playing

"Outside Playing" is a catch-all term that refers to the prominent use of scale tones that lie outside the standard key—those "clashing" tones in particular. Example 147 shows a descending tapping portion from my solo to "My Funk" (*Exottica*, 2000) that oozes with chromatics. The riff underneath implies Em pentatonic, and the lead focuses primarily on E and B (1–5) with an added F (♭2). Then all the chromatic tones in between are also used. Are we having fun yet?!

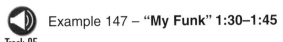

Example 147 – "My Funk" 1:30–1:45

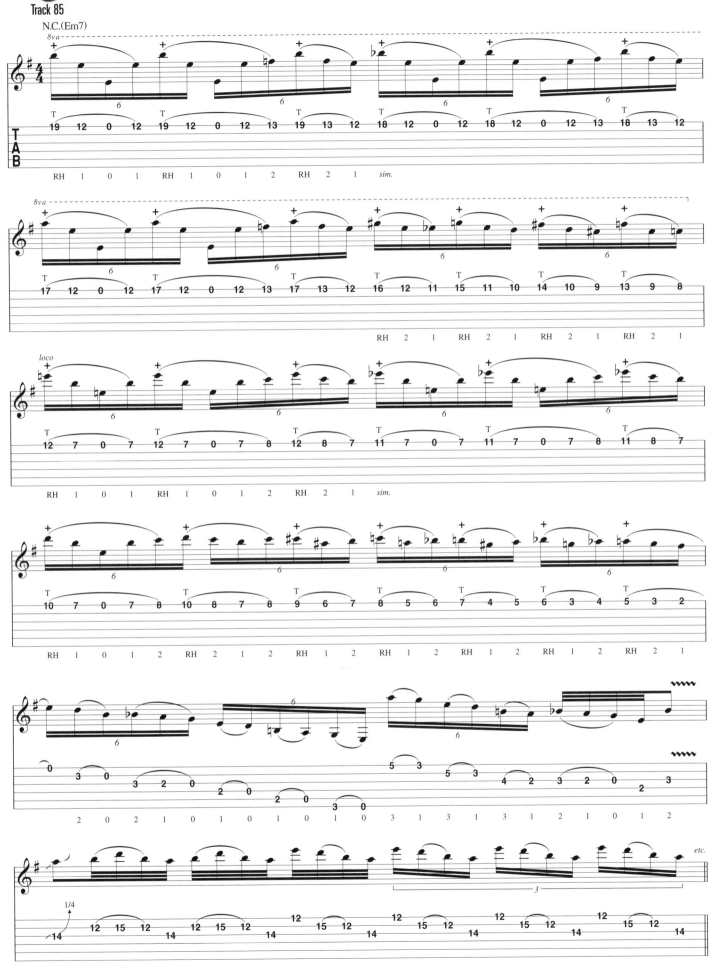

We can even take the idea of outside tones further by building larger structures of "embellishment patterns" and moving these entire patterns outside the key temporarily. For example, in the middle of a fast blues run, drop a pattern of say four or eight notes one fret and repeat. All the notes will be out of key, but don't sweat it! Drop it another fret and repeat. You're still out of key. Now up a fret. Still out. Up again and you finally rejoin "solid ground." Play this fast enough and it will sound curiously interesting. Because you come back and make sense, the out of key moment is "forgiven."

Example 148 shows a descending half-diminished arpeggio, taken chromatically right down the neck. Here the out of key notes last more than a moment, but similarly, they eventually join up with the original key and we land "on our feet."

Track 86

Example 148 – "**Exottica**" 0:35–0:58

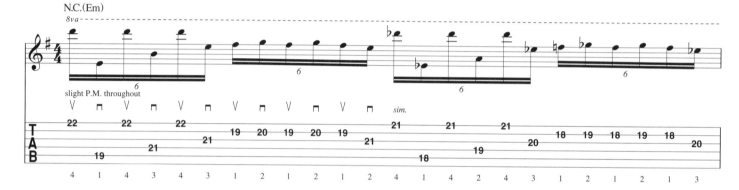

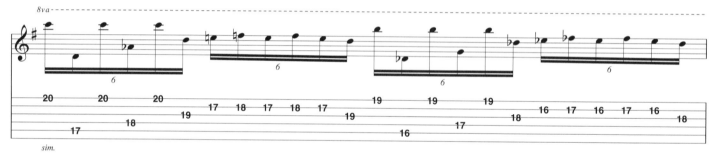

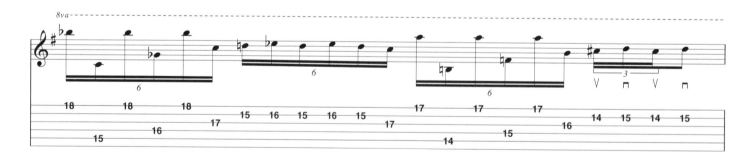

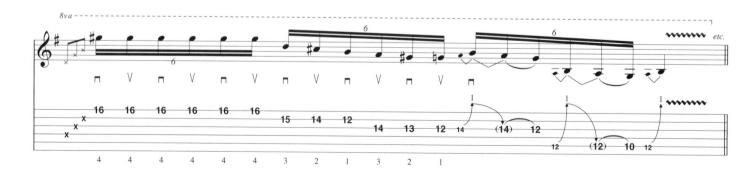

Example 149 is the main solo from "Exottica." It is chock full of outside playing, parallel tonality, and pitch axis techniques.

Track 87

Example 149 – "Exottica" 2:00–2:24

"Sunrise" (Exottica, 2000)

The instrumental tune "Sunrise" is the final track from my *Exottica* album. It is also a good wrap-up to apply the material of this book. The song is in E♭ slack tuning, so you will need to tune accordingly. The low E♭ note is sounded on CD track 88 as a tuning reference if needed.

Track 88 E♭ Slack Tuning – Low E string

First, listen to the song to familiarize yourself with the parts generally. Identify the tonal center and the overall progressions by ear. Then find those chording parts on the guitar and play along. Next, tackle the melodies. Listen to them and try to identify the significant tones in play, also by ear. Then play these melodies too, noting how they interact with the underlying chords. After taking a shot at it by ear, refer to the transcription of "Sunrise' in the appendix to see how well you did.

Finally, take a crack at the solos. The first step here is to familiarize yourself with them to the point that you can replay them in your mind and "hear" the whole thing. Take the first phrase, identify the tones by ear one at a time, and play them on the fretboard to check yourself. At first you may need to do this one note at a time—listen up to that note and hit the pause button. Fast runs are difficult to learn by ear. However, the better you get at this, the more notes you can do at once—recognizing full runs, familiar licks, and scales by ear. Still, learning "outside" licks and extremely fast runs can require slowing down the recording, etc. It's not necessary to go that far. After you learn as much of these solos as possible, simply refer to the transcription to check your work and learn the fastest runs.

> TIP: One word about the uneven note-groupings in the solos: These are often not felt as directly connected to the beat. (Although in some cases, groups of 5 notes may be.) They are more often the result of "going for it"—cramming notes into the phrase and then coming out in time by feeling the impending end of the phrase. A good case in point is the ascending run in measures 25–26. It loses connection with the underlying pulse, yet comes out in time as it hits the final high D note and rejoins with rhythm. To practice these sorts of runs, you are better off to break them apart based on their pattern groupings (not rhythmically-based groupings). Repeat these shapes using whatever rhythm is convenient. Then string them all together and "go for it!" Good luck!

Example 150 – **"Sunrise"**

Track 89

APPENDIX I – Transcriptions

Example 25

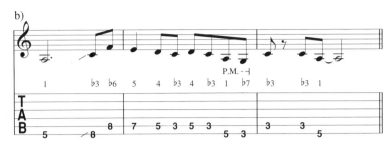

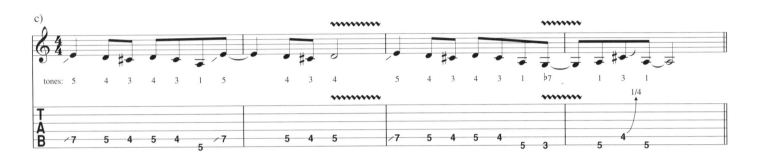

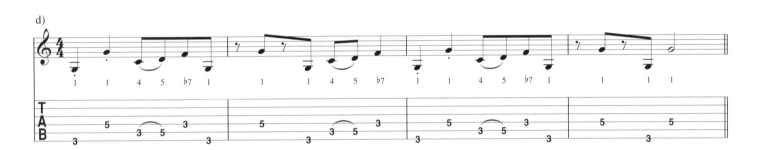

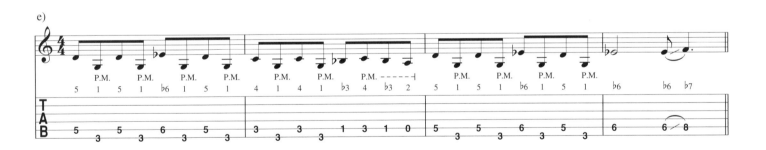

g)

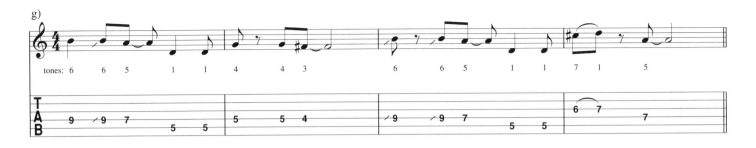

h)

i)

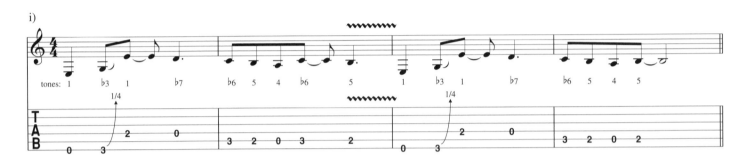

Example 27

(with octaves)

b)

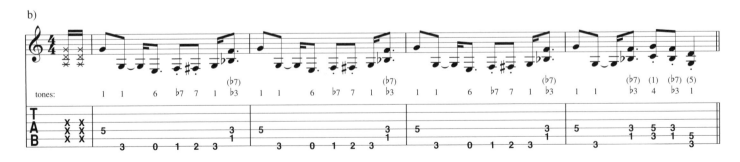

Example 41

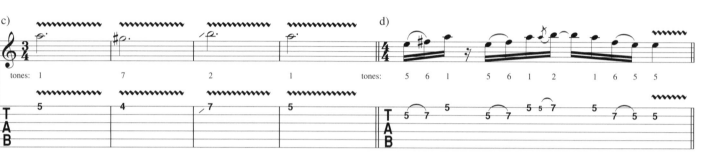

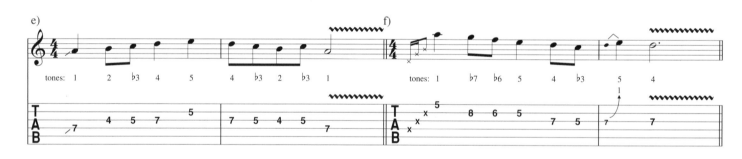

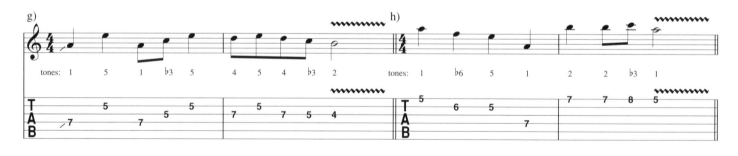

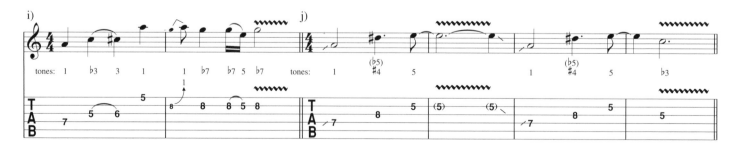

138

Example 45

139

Example 46

a)

b)

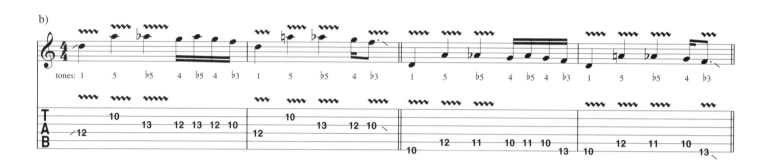

c)

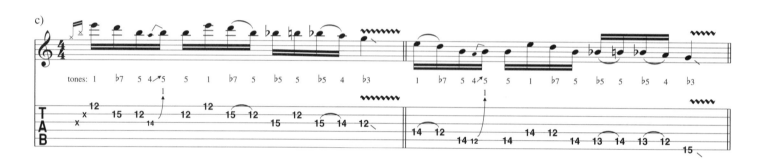

Example 49

Dorian melody:

Phrygian melody:

Lydian melody:

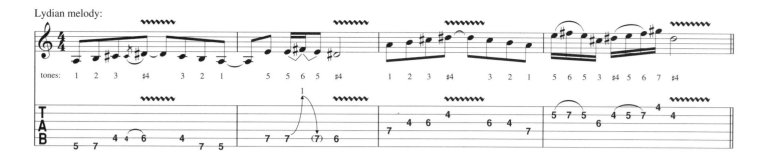

tones: 1 2 3 #4 3 2 1 5 5 6 5 #4 1 2 3 #4 3 2 1 5 6 5 3 #4 5 6 7 #4

Mixolydian melody:

let ring throughout

tones: 1 3 4 5 4 3 1 3 1 ♭7 ♭7 ♭7 6 1 6 6 5 1 5

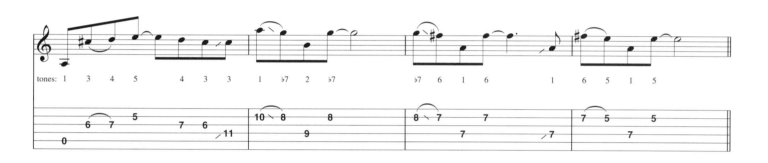

tones: 1 3 4 5 4 3 3 1 ♭7 2 ♭7 ♭7 6 1 6 1 6 5 1 5

Locrian melody:

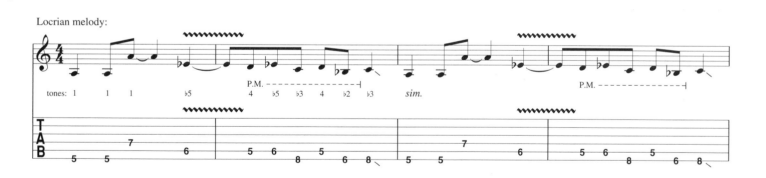

tones: 1 1 1 ♭5 4 ♭5 ♭3 4 ♭2 ♭3 *sim.*

P.M. - - - - - - - - - - - - - - - -   P.M. - - - - - - - - - - - - - - -

P.M. - - - - - - - - - - - -   P.M. - - - - - - - - - - - -

Example 51

a)

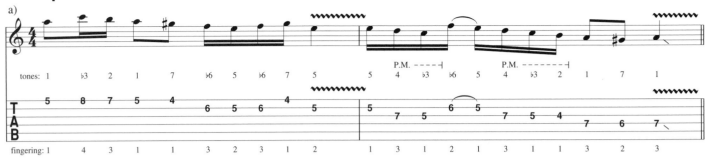

b)

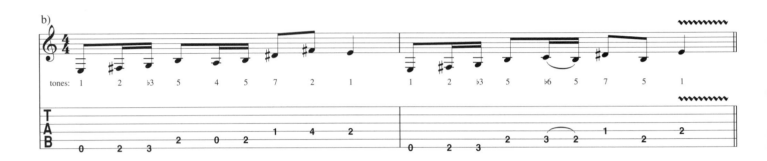

Example 52

a)

b)

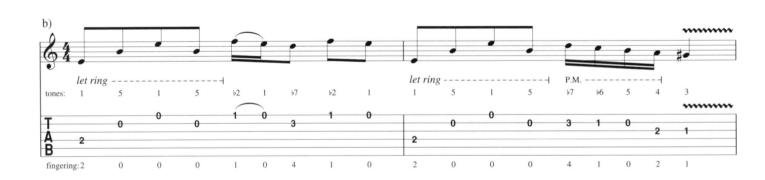

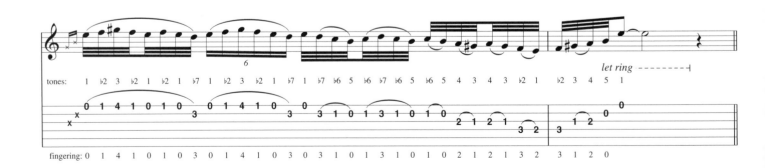

Example 53

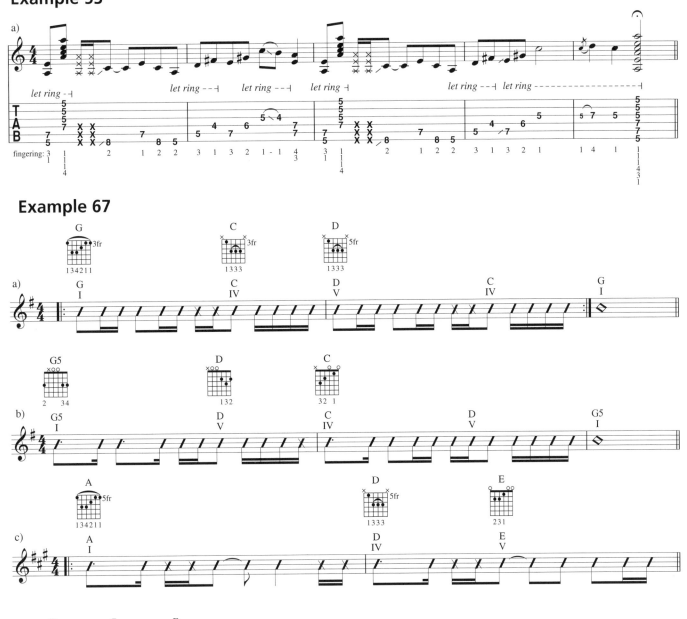

Example 67

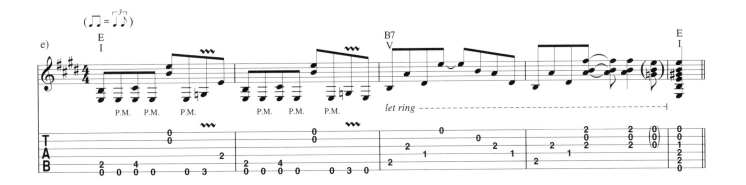

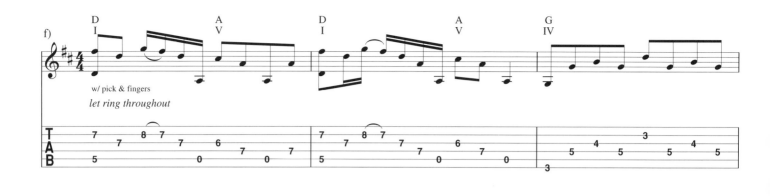

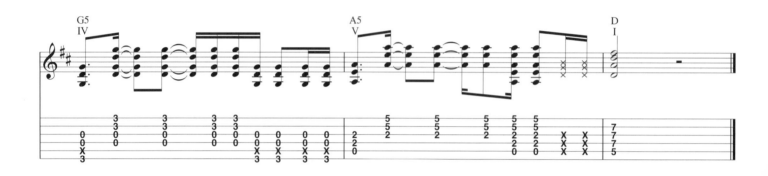

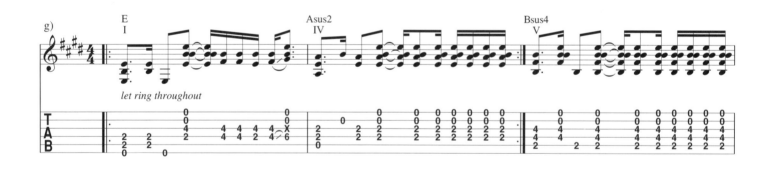

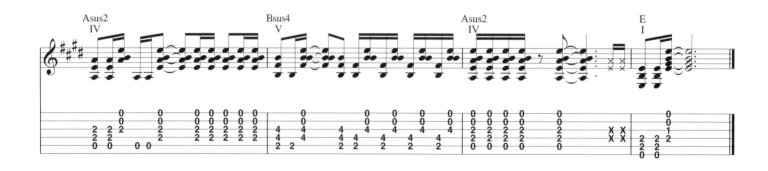

Example 68

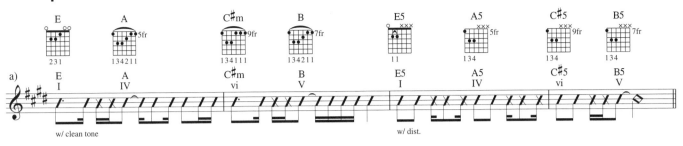

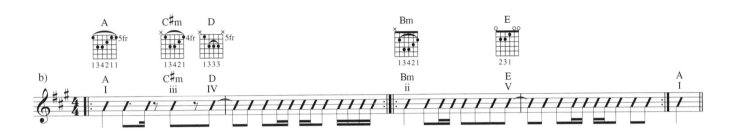

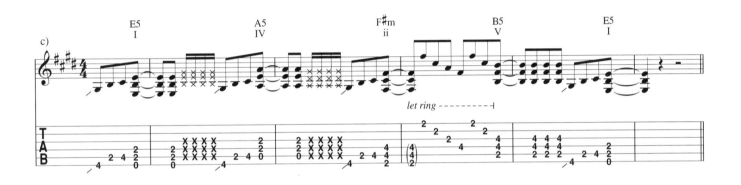

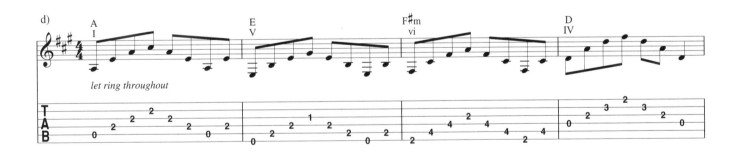

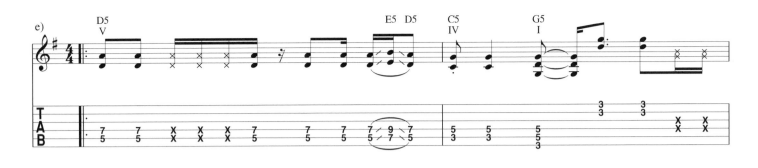

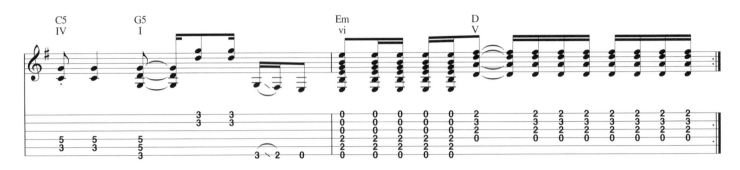

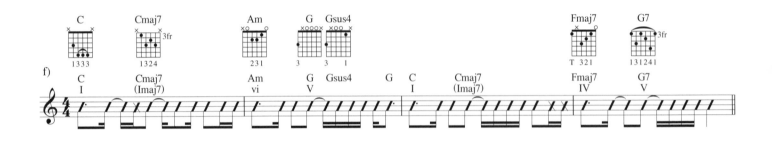

Example 69

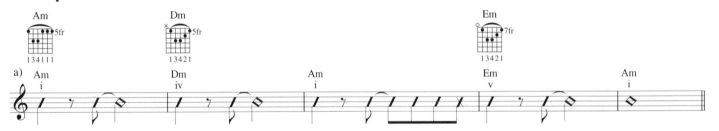

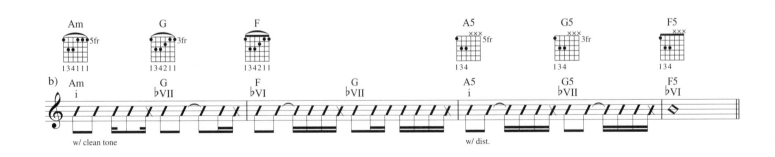

Example 71

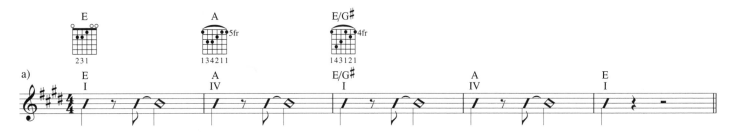

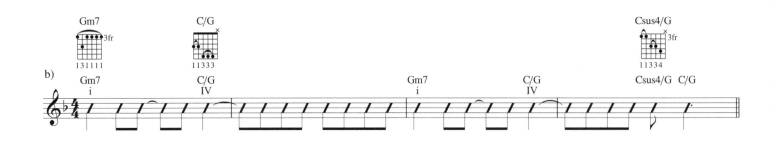

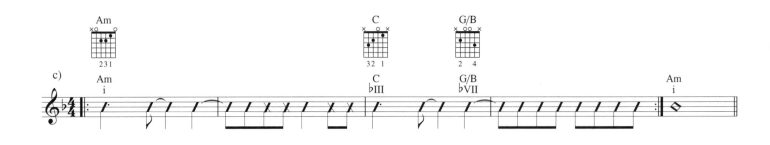

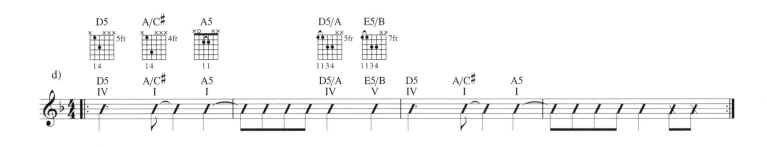

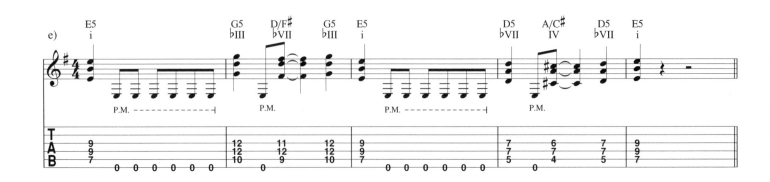

Example 77

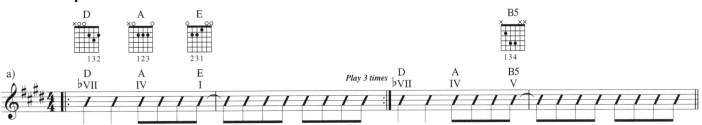

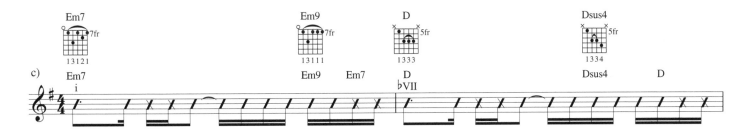

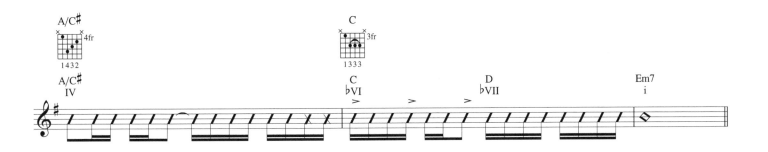

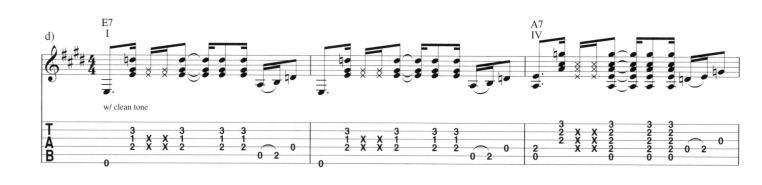

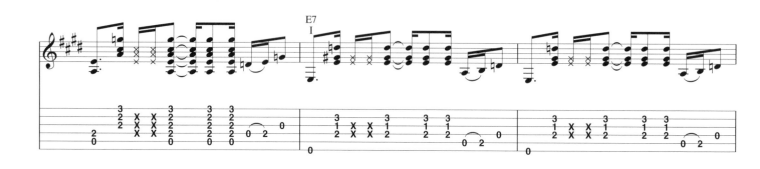

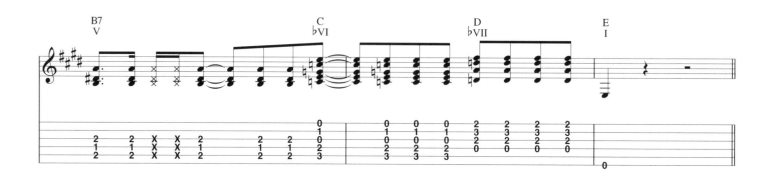

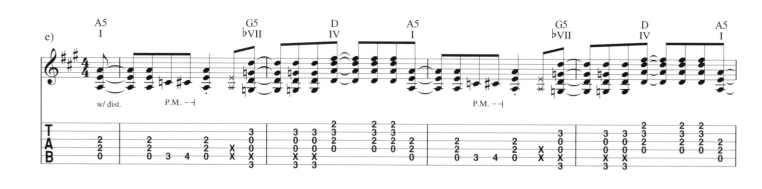

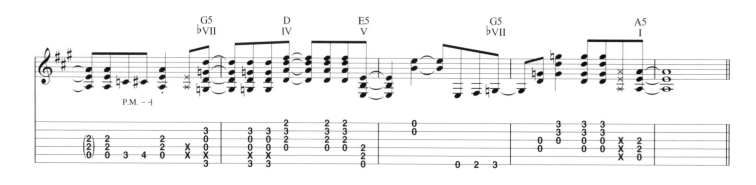

SUNRISE

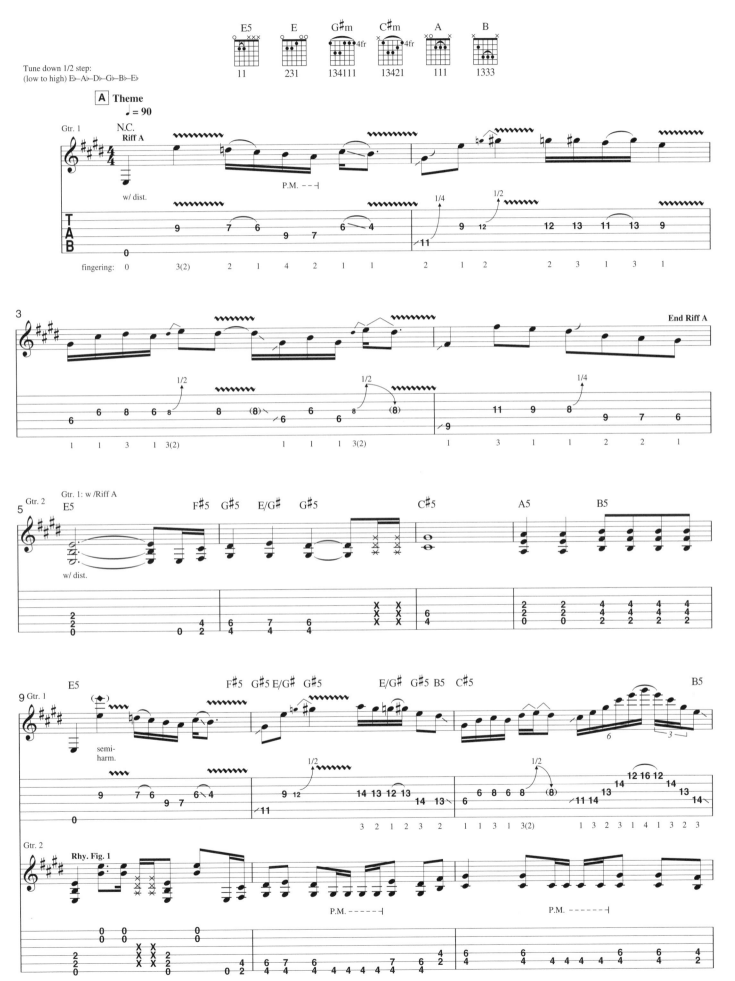

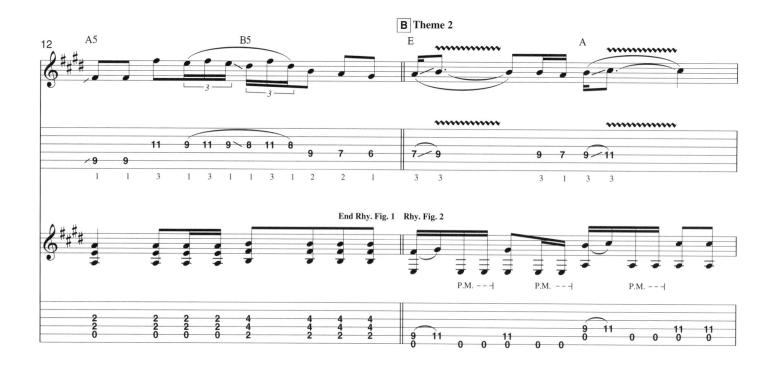

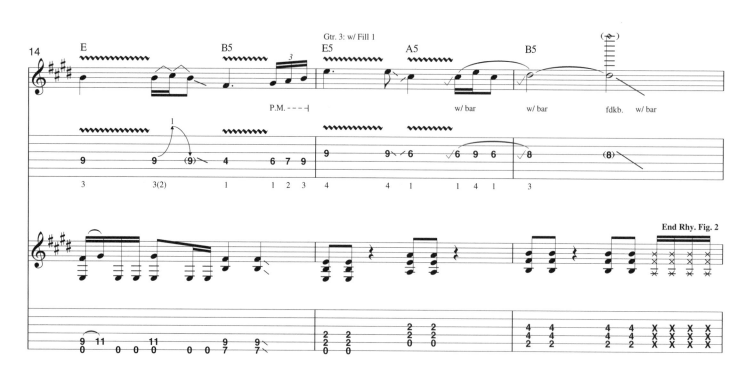

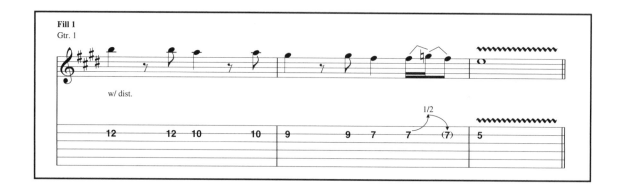

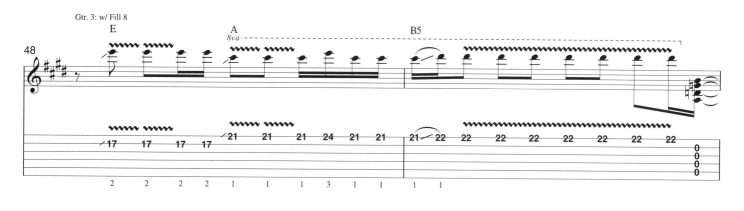

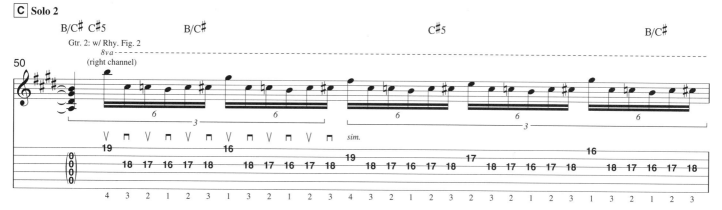

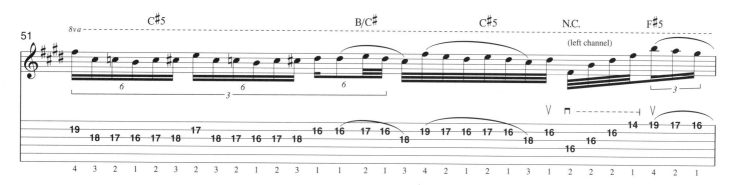

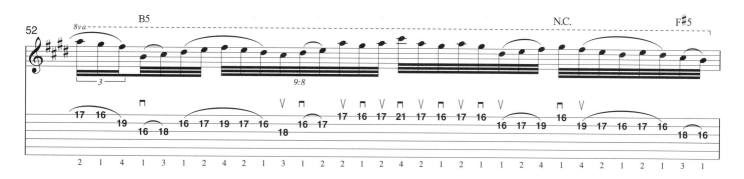

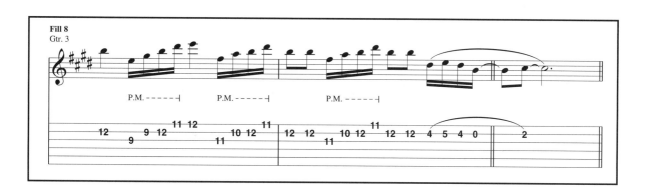

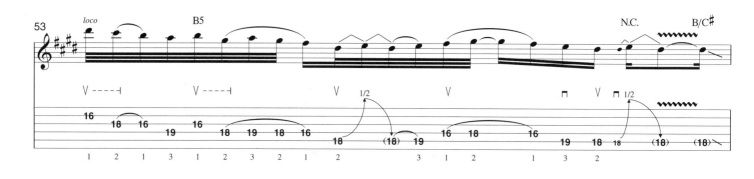

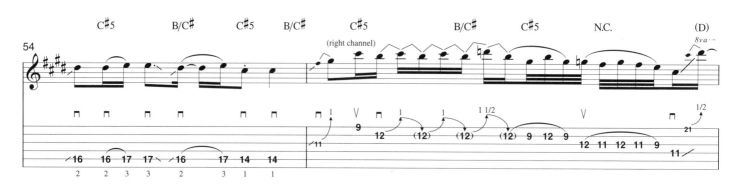

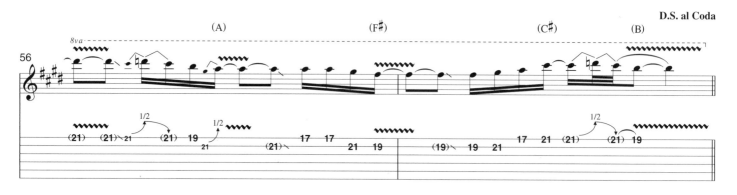

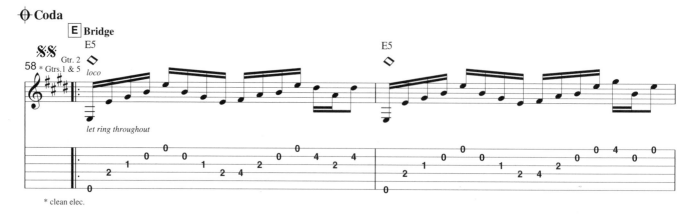

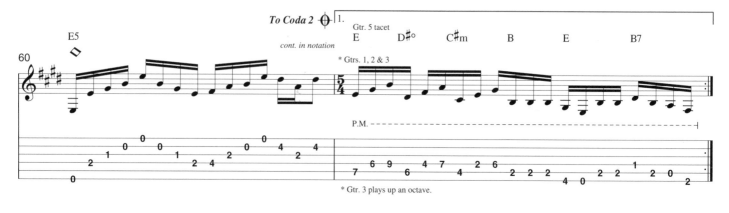

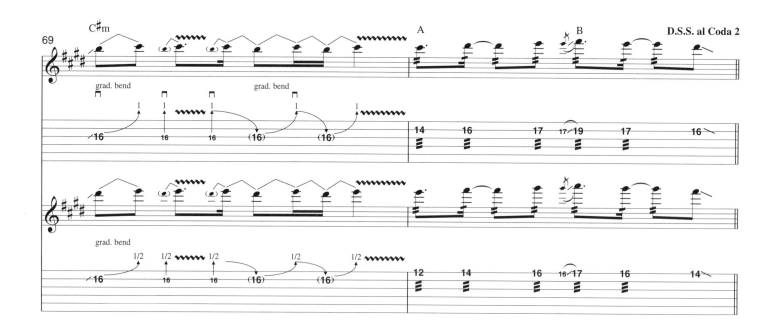

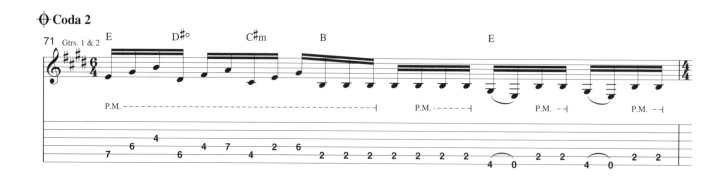

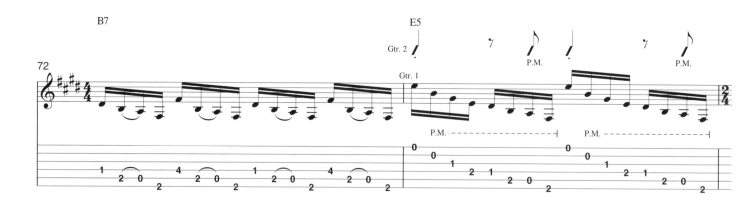

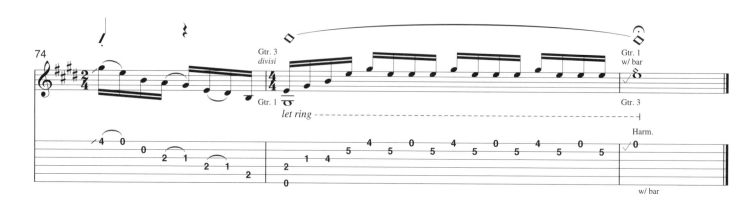

ANSWERS

Ex. 2 Answers:

maj 3rd, 5th, maj 6th, octave, maj 2nd, 4th, maj 7th, unison

Ex. 5 Answers:
a) octave
b) maj 6th
c) maj 7th
d) maj 3rd
e) 5th
f) 4th
g) unison
h) maj 2nd
i) maj 7th
j) 4th
k) maj 6th
l) octave
m) 5th
n) maj 3rd
o) maj 7th
p) maj 2nd
q) maj 6th

Ex. 8 Answers:
a) Maj 3rd
b) 5th
c) maj 7th
d) 4th
e) unison
f) maj 6th
g) maj 2nd
h) maj 3rd
i) 5th
j) octave

Ex. 15 Answers:
a) min 6th
b) min 3rd
c) min 3rd
d) min 7th
e) min 2nd
f) min 3rd
g) min 3rd
h) min 2nd
i) min 7th

Ex. 20 Answers:
a) major
b) minor
c) diminished
d) augmented
e) minor
f) major
g) major
h) diminished
i) minor
j) augmented
k) minor
l) major
m) minor
n) diminished
o) minor
p) major
q) minor
r) major
s) augmented

Ex. 21 Answers:
a) 1-3-5-8
b) 1-♭3-5-8
c) 1-3-8-5
d) 8-5-3-1
e) 1-♭3-3-1
f) 1-♭3-8-♭3
g) 5-♭3-1-5
h) ♭3-1-5-1
i) 8-5-3-1
j) 3-1-5-1
k) 5-♭3-8-1
l) 8-5-3-8
m) 8-5-3-1
n) 5-8-1-3

Ex. 23 Answers:
a) 1-2-1
b) 3-4-3
c) 5-♭6-5
d) ♭3-4-5
e) 5-♯4-5-6-5-1
f) 1-7-1-2-3
g) 1-3-5-♭6-5
h) 5-♭6-♭7-1-5-♭3-1
i) 5-♭3-1-2-♭3-4-♭3
j) 4-3-2-3-2
k) 1-1-♭5-4-1
l) 1-3-2-1-5-4-3
m) 1-3-4-6-5-7-1
n) 1-♭3-3-1-♭7-5-♭7

Ex. 24 Answers:
a) D, C, D
b) D, C, C, C
c) D, D, C, D
d) D, D, C, C, C
e) C, C, D, D, C, C
f) D, C, C, D, D, C, D, C
g) C, D, D, C, D, C, C, C, C

Ex. 25 Answers:
a) 1-♭3-4-♭3-1-♭7 | 5-♭7-1
b) 1-♭3-♭6 | 5-4-♭3-4-♭3-1-♭7 | ♭3-♭3-1
c) 5-4-3-4-3-1-5 | 4-3-4 | 5-4-3-4-3-1-♭7 | 1-3-1
d) 1-1-4-5-♭7-1 | 1-1-4-5-♭7 | 1-1-4-5-♭7-1 | 1-1-1
e) 5-1-5-1-♭6-1-5-1 | 4-1-4-1-♭3-4-♭3-2 | 5-1-5-1-♭6-1-5-1 | ♭6-♭6-♭7
f) 1-1 | 3-4-5-♭7-1-1 | 3-4-3-1-1-1 | 3-4-5-♭7-1-1 | 1-♭7-1
g) 6-6-5-1-1 | 4-4-3 | 6-6-5-1-1 | 7-1-5
h) 3-1-♭7-1-1 | 3-1-♭7 | 3-1-♭7-4-4-3 | 1-♭7
i) 1-♭3-1-♭7-♭6-5-4-♭6-5 | 1-♭3-1-♭7-♭6-5-4-5

Ex. 27 Answers:
a) 1-♭3-1-♭7-7 | 1-♭3-1-♭7-7 | 1-♭3-1-♭7-7 | 1-♭3-4-♭3 | (repeat adding octaves to each note)
b) 1-1-6-♭7-7-1-♭3 | 1-1-6-♭7-7-1-♭3 | 1-1-6-♭7-7-1-♭3 | 1-1-♭3-4-♭3-1 (adding 5ths to final ♭3-4-♭3-1)
c) 1-1-♭7-6-♭6 | 1-1-5-♭5-4 | 1-1-♭7-6-♭6 | 1-1-4-♭5-5-5-♭5-4-♭3-4-♭3 | 1 (adding 5ths to final ♭3-4-♭3-1)
d) 1-5-1-♭6-5-5-5 | 1-5-1-♯4-5-5-5 | 1-5-1-♭6-5-5-5 | 1-2-♭3-2-♭2 (adding octaves on 5 & ♭6 throughout, adding 5ths on the last two notes)
e) 1-1-♭7 | 1-♭7-6 | 1-6-♭6 | 1-1-♭3-♭3-4-4-♭5-5-♭5-5 (adding 5ths on ending, 2nd time)
f) 1-1-3-3-4-4-♭5-♭5-5-5-♭5-♭5-4-4-3-3 | 1-1-1-♭3-3-1-♭7-♭7-5-♭7-7 | 1-1-1 (ends on A7)
g) ♭7-1-1-♭2-1-1-♭7-1-1 | ♭7-1-1-♭3-1-1-♭7-1-1 | ♭7-1-1-♭2-1-1-♭7-1-1 | ♭7-1-1-♭3-1-1-5-♭5-4-♭3 (adding 5ths to all notes except ♭7, ♭2, and ending 5-♭5-4-♭3, which are single notes)

Ex. 32 Answers:

Ex. 39 Answers:

161

Ex. 41 Answers:

    a) 1 | 5-6-5 | 1 1 | 3-4-3-2 | 3

    b) 2 | 2-2-1-2-3 | 4-3-2 | 1

    c) 1 | 7 | 2 | 1

    d) 5-6-1-5-6-1-2-1-6-5-5

    e) 1-2-♭3-4-5 | 4-♭3-2-♭3-1

    f) 1-♭7-♭6-5-4-♭3 | 5-4

    g) 1-5-1-♭3-5 | 4-5-4-♭3-2

    h) 1-♭6-5-1 | 2-2-♭3-1

    i) 1-♭3-3-1 | 1-♭7-♭7-5-♭7

    j) 1-♯4-5 | 1-♯4-5 | ♭3

Ex. 43 Answers:

    a) A7:   1-5-♭7-3-5-1

    b) Am7:   1-5-♭7-♭3-5-1

    c) Amaj7:   1-3-5-7

    d) Amaj7:   1-5-7-3-5

    e) Am(maj7):   1-5-1-♭3-7

    f) Am7:   1-♭3-♭7-1

    g) Amaj7:   1-5-7-3

    h) A7:   1-3-♭7-1

    i) Am7:   1-5-1-♭3-♭7

    j) A7:   1-5-♭7-3-♭7-1

    k) A7:   1-5-♭7-3-5

    l) Am7:   1-5-♭7-♭3-♭7-1

    m) Am7:   1-5-♭7-♭3-5

    n) Amaj7:   1-7-3-5

    o) Am(maj7):   1-7-♭3-5

    p) Am(maj7):   1-♭3-5-7

    q) Amaj7:   1-5-1-3-7

    r) A7:   1-5-1-3-♭7

    s) Am(maj7):   1-7-♭3-5

Ex. 45 Answers:

    a) 1-♭3-4-♭3-1 | 5-4-♭3-1

    b) 1-♭7-5-♭7-5-♭3-1

    c) 5-4 ↑5-4-♭3 ↑4-♭3

    d) 1-5-♭7-1-♭3-1

    e) 1-♭7-5-1-♭7-4

    f) 1-♭3-♭3 ↑ 4-4 ↓♭3 | 1-♭3-♭3 ↑4-4 ↑ 5

    g) ♭7 ↑1-♭3-♭7 ↑1-♭7-5-♭7 ↑1

    h) 1-♭7-5 | 5-4-♭3-1

    i) 1-♭3-♭7-1

Ex. 46 Answers:

    a) 1-♭3-4-♭5-4-♭3 | 1

    b) 1-5-♭5-4-♭5-4-♭3 | 1-5-♭5-4-♭3

    c) 1-♭7-5-4 ↑5-5-1-♭7-5-♭5-5-♭5-4-♭3

Ex. 51 Answers:

    a) 1-♭3-2-1-7-♭6-5-♭6-7-5
        | 5-4-♭3-♭6-5-4-♭3-2-1-7-1

    b) 1-2-♭3-5-4-5-7-2-1 | 1-2-♭3-5-♭6-5-7-5-1

Ex. 52 Answers:

    a) 1-♭2-3-4-5-♭6-5-4-3 | ♭2-1-5-1
        | 1-♭2-3-4-5-♭6-5-4 | 3-♭2-1

    b) 1-5-1-5-♭2-1-♭7-♭2-1 1-5-1-5-♭7-♭6-5-4-3
        1-♭2-3-♭2-1-♭7-1-♭7-♭6-5-♭6-♭7-♭6-5-♭6-5-
        4-3-4-3-♭2-1-♭2-3-4-5-1

Ex. 53 Answer:

    a) 1-1-♭3-5-♭3-1 | 4-6-5-7-♭3-2-1
        | 1-1-♭3-5-♭3-1 | 4-6-5-7-♭3 | 4-♭3-1

Ex. 59 Answers:

    a) C major

    b) G major

    c) F major

    d) E major

    e) D major

    f) B♭ major

    g) B major

    h) A major

Ex. 67 Answers:

    a) I-IV | V-IV | I-IV | V-IV | I (up to IV and V)

    b) I-V | IV-V | I (up to IV and V)

    c) I | IV-V | I | IV-V (down to V)

    d) I-V | IV | I-V | IV-V | I (down to V and IV)

    e) I | I | I | V | V | I (with blues comping embellishment)

    f) I-V | I-V | IV | V (repeat with distortion)

    g) I | IV | I | IV | V | IV | V | IV | I
        (with open string common tones)

Ex. 68 Answers:

    a) I-IV | vi-V (and with distortion: I5-IV5 | vi5-V5)

    b) I-iii | IV | I-iii | IV | ii | V | ii | V | I

    c) I5 | IV5 | ii | V5 | I5

    d) I | V | vi | IV | I | V | IV-iii-ii | I

    e) V5 | IV5-I5 | IV5-I5 | vi-V

    f) I-Imaj7 | vi-V | I-Imaj7 | IVmaj7-V7

Ex. 69 Answers:

    a) i | iv | i | v | i

    b) i-♭VII | ♭VI-♭VII | i5-♭VII5 | ♭VI5

    c) i5 | ♭VI5 | i | ♭VI5-♭VII5 | i

    d) i5 | ♭III5-iv5 | i5 | ♭III5-♭VII5

    e) i5 | ♭VI5 | ♭III5 | ♭VII5 | i5 | ♭VI | ♭III5 | ♭VII

    f) i-♭III5 | i-♭III5 | i-♭III5 | IV-V | i

    g) i5-♭VI5 | IV | i5-♭VI5 | IV

    h) i | ♭VI-V | i | i | ♭VI-V

Ex. 71 Answers:

    a) I | IV | I₃ | IV | I

    b) i | IV₅ | i | IV₅

    c) i | i | i | ♭III | ♭VII₃ | i | i | i | ♭III | ♭VII₃ | i

    d) IV5-I₃-I5 | IV5₅-V5₅ | IV5-I₃-I

    e) i | ♭III5-♭VII₃-♭III5 | i | i | ♭VII5-IV₃-♭VII5 | i

Ex. 77 Answers:

    a) ♭VII-IV | I | I | ♭VII-IV | I | I | ♭VII-IV | I | I | ♭VII-IV | V

    b) I | I | ♭VI | I | I | V | I | I | ♭VI | ♭III | ♭II | I

    c) i | I | ♭VII | IV₃ | ♭VI-♭VII | i

    d) I | I | I | IV | IV | I | I | I | V | ♭VI-♭VII | I

    e) I | I | ♭VII-IV | I | I | ♭VII-IV | I | I | ♭VII-IV | V | ♭VII | I

Ex. 79g answers:

    1) 7-4, 1-3

    2) 5-7-4, 5-1-3

    3) 7-4-♭6, 1-3-5

    4) 7-4-6, 1-3-5

    5) 7-4-♭6-2, 1-3-5-1

    6) 7-4-6-2, 1-3-5-1

    7) 5-7-4-6-2, 1-5-1-3-5-1

    8) 7-4-♭6-2, 1-3-5-1

    9) 2-4-7-♭3, 1-5-1-3

Ex. 90 answers :

Measure 1-2:	5-4-3-1 │ 5-4-♭3-1
Measure 3-4:	5-4 4-♭3 5/♭7-4/6 4-♭3 │ 5-5-1-♭7-5 5-♭5-4-♭3-4-5 1
Measure 5-6:	3-4-5-3-4-5-3-1 │ ♭3-4-5-♭3-♭6-5-♭3/5
Measure 7-8:	1-♭3-6-♭3-4-6 │ ♭7-6-♭3
Measure 9-10:	5-5-1-5-5-1-5-5-1-5-4-♭3-4-♭3-4-♭3 │ 5-4-♭3-1-4-1-♭3-1-♭7-1-♭3-1
Measure 11-12:	3-3-3-2-2-2-3-3-3-1-1-1-3-3-1-1 │ ♭3-♭3-♭3-2-2-2-♭3-♭3-♭3-2-2-2-1
Measure 13:	1-1-1-1 1-1-1-1 1-2-1-1 1-1-1-1
Measure 14:	♭7-♭7-♭7-♭7 ♭7-♭7-♭7-♭7 ♭7-1-♭7-♭7 ♭7-♭7-♭7-♭7
Measure 15-16:	6-4-6-4-6-4 │ ♭7-6-4-♭7-6
Measure 17-18:	1 │ ♭7
Measure 19-20:	6 │ 5-4-♭3-1 4/6-1-♭3/5-1 ♭7-5-♭5-4 ♭5-4
Measure 21:	1

Ex. 91 answers:

Measure 1-4:	1-5-♭7-4 │ 5-♭3-1-1
Measure 5-8:	1-5-♭7-4 │ 5-♭3-1-1
Measure 9:	1-♭7-5-♭7-5-♭5 5-♭5-4-♭5-4-♭3 ♭7-5-♭5-♭3-4-♭5 ♭7-5-♭5-♭3-4-♭5
Measure 10:	5-♭5-♭3-4-♭3-1 ♭3-1-♭7-1-♭7-5 ♭5-4-♭3-1-♭3-4 ♭5-4-♭3-4-♭3-1
Measure 11:	♭3-1-♭7-1-♭3-4 ♭5-4-♭3-4-♭3-1 ♭3-1-♭3-♭5-♭3-♭5 6-♭5-6-1-6-1
Measure 12:	♭3-1-6-1-♭3-1-6 1-♭3-1 ♭3-4-♭5-5-6-♭7 1-2-♭3-4
Measure 13-16:	5-4-♭3-1 ♭3-1↑2 │ ↑♭3-3 ♭3 ♭3 2-1-♭7-5 ♭7-1-5-4-♭3-1
Measure 17-20:	1-1-1-♭7 ♭7-♭7-♭7-1-2-♭3 4-4-♭3-5-4 ♭3-1-1
Measure 21-22:	♭3/5-♭3/5-♭3/5 ♭7-6-5-6-5-4-♭3 5-1 (1)

Ex. 94c answers :

C-C$_3$-C$_5$-C   C-Dm-C │ F-Em-Dm-C

Ex. 115 answers:

a) 5-5-1 ♭7-5-♭6-5-4 5-5-4-♭3-1 4-♭3-2-♭3 │ 2 1-2 │ ♭3-2-1-♭7-1-♭7-♭6-5 ♭6-♭7-♭6-5-♭6-5-4-♭3 2-♭3-2-1-2-♭3 1

b) ♭7-1-1 │ 1 4-5-♭6-5-♭6-5-4 ♭3-1-2-♭3-2-1 2-1-♭7-1-♭7-♭6 │ 5-♭6-♭7-♭6-5-4 5-4-♭3-2-♭3-4 5-♭3 1

c) 1-♭3-5-♭7-5-♭3 1 1 │ 5-♭6-5-4 5-4-♭3-2 ♭3-4-♭3-2 ♭3-2-1-♭7 │ ♭3-1 1 │ 1-2-♭3-4-5-♭6 5-4-♭3-2-1-♭7
│ ♭6-5-♭6-♭7-1-♭6-5

d) 1-♭3-1-2-1-♭7 1-♭3-1-2-1-♭7 1-♭7-♭6-5-♭6-5-4 5-5-5 │ 5-♭6-♭7-1-2-♭3 4-♭3-2-1-2-♭3 4-5-♭6-5-♭6-♭7 1-1

Ex. 138 answers:

A blues-natural minor   A Dorian-Mixolydian   A major-minor

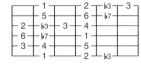

Ex. 145 answers:

Root = A   Root = C   Root = E

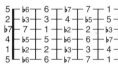  

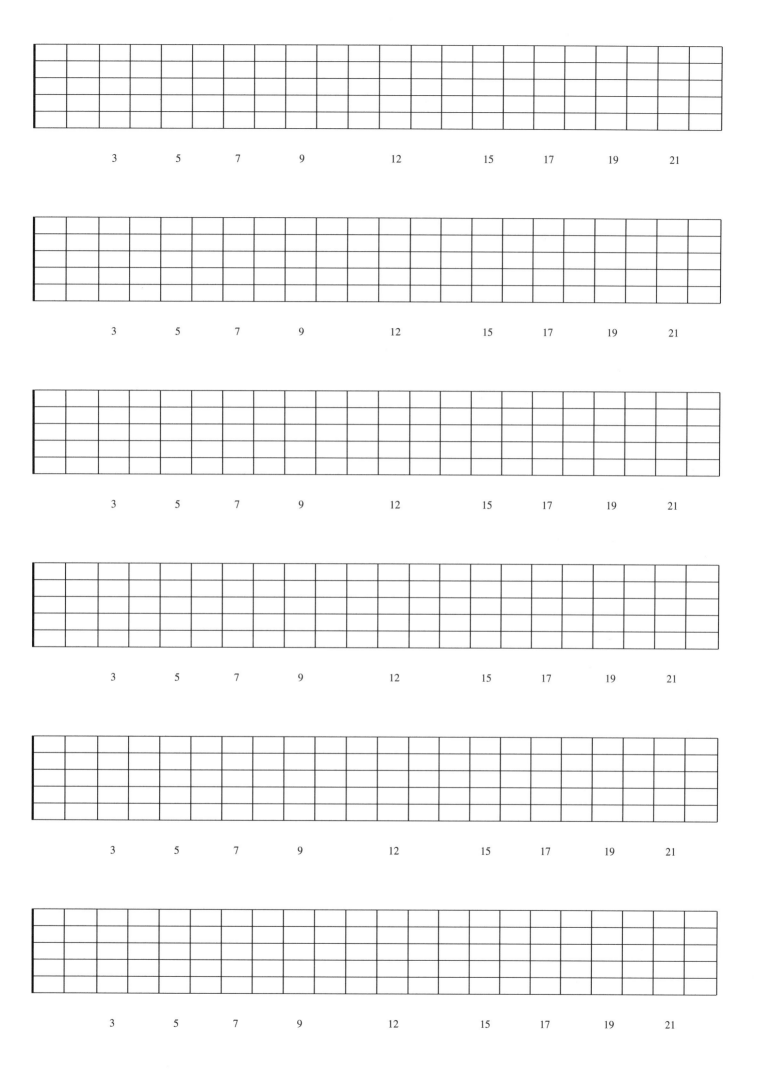

0207

HAL LEONARD GUITAR METHOD BOOK 1
SECOND EDITION
CD INCLUDED
BY WILL SCHMID AND GREG KOCH

HAL LEONARD GUITAR METHOD

THE HAL LEONARD GUITAR METHOD is designed for anyone just learning to play acoustic or electric guitar. It is based on years of teaching guitar students of all ages, and it also reflects some of the best guitar teaching ideas from around the world. This comprehensive method includes: Learning sequence carefully paced with clear instructions; popular songs which increase the incentive to learn to play; versatility – can be used as self-instruction or with a teacher; audio accompaniments so that students have fun and sound great while practicing.

BOOK 1

Book 1 provides beginning instruction which includes tuning, playing position, musical symbols, notes in first position, the C, G, G7, D, D7, A7, and Em chords, rhythms through eighth notes, strumming and picking, 100 great songs, riffs, and examples. Includes a chord chart and well-known songs: Ode to Joy • Rockin' Robin • Greensleeves • Give My Regards to Broadway • Time Is on My Side.
00699010 Book $5.95
00699027 Book/CD Pack $9.95

BOOK 2

Book 2 continues the instruction started in Book 1 and covers: Am, Dm, A, E, F and B7 chords; power chords; finger-style guitar; syncopations, dotted rhythms, and triplets; Carter style solos; bass runs; pentatonic scales; improvising; tablature; 92 great songs, riffs and examples; notes in first and second position; and more! The CD includes 57 full-band tracks.
00699020 Book $5.95
00697313 Book/CD Pack $9.95

BOOK 3

Book 3 covers: the major, minor, pentatonic, and chromatic scales, sixteenth notes; barre chords; drop D tuning; movable scales; notes in fifth position; slides, hammer-ons, pull-offs, and string bends; chord construction; gear; 90 great songs, riffs, and examples; and more! The CD includes 61 full-band tracks.
00699030 Book $5.95
00697316 Book/CD Pack $9.95

COMPOSITE

Books 1, 2, and 3 bound together in an easy-to-use spiral binding.
00699040 Books Only $14.95
00697342 Book/3-CD Pack $22.95

VIDEO AND DVD

FOR THE BEGINNING ELECTRIC OR ACOUSTIC GUITARIST
00697318 DVD $19.95
00320159 VHS Video $14.95
00697341 Book/CD Pack and DVD $24.95

SONGBOOKS

EASY POP RHYTHMS

Strum along with your favorite hits from the Beatles, the Rolling Stones, the Eagles and more!
00697336 Book $5.95
00697309 Book/CD Pack $14.95

MORE EASY POP RHYTHMS

00697338 Book $5.95
00697322 Book/CD Pack...........................$14.95

EVEN MORE EASY POP RHYTHMS

00697340 Book $5.95
00697323 Book/CD Pack...........................$14.95

EASY POP MELODIES

Play along with your favorite hits from the Beatles, Elton John, Elvis Presley, the Police, Nirvana, and more!
00697281 Book $5.95
00697268 Book/CD Pack...........................$14.95

MORE EASY POP MELODIES

00697280 Book $5.95
00697269 Book/CD Pack...........................$14.95

EVEN MORE EASY POP MELODIES

00699154 Book $5.95
00697270 Book/CD Pack...........................$14.95

LEAD LICKS

Over 200 licks in all styles.
00697345 Book/CD Pack...........................$9.95

RHYTHM RIFFS

Over 200 riffs in all styles.
00697346 Book/CD Pack...........................$9.95

STYLISTIC METHODS

ACOUSTIC GUITAR

by Chad Johnson

This book uses real songs to teach you the basics of acoustic guitar in the styles of The Beatles, The Rolling Stones, Eric Clapton, Robert Johnson, and many others.
00697347 Book/CD Pack.........................$14.95

BLUES GUITAR

by Greg Koch

This book teaches the basics of blues guitar in the style of B.B. King, Stevie Ray Vaughan, Buddy Guy, Muddy Waters, and more.
00697326 Book/CD Pack.........................$12.95

COUNTRY GUITAR

by Greg Koch

This book teaches the basics of country guitar in the styles of Chet Atkins, Albert Lee, Merle Travis and more.
00697337 Book/CD Pack.........................$12.95

JAZZ GUITAR

by Jeff Schroedl

This book teaches the basics of jazz guitar in the style of Wes Montgomery, Joe Pass, Tal Farlow, Charlie Christian, Jim Hall, and more.
00695359 Book/CD Pack.........................$12.95

ROCK GUITAR

by Michael Mueller

This book teaches the basics of rock guitar in the style of Eric Clapton, the Beatles, the Rolling Stones, and many others.
00697319 Book/CD Pack.........................$12.95

REFERENCE

ARPEGGIO FINDER

AN EASY-TO-USE GUIDE TO OVER 1,300 GUITAR ARPEGGIOS

00697352 6" x 9" Edition $4.95
00697351 9" x 12" Edition $5.95

INCREDIBLE CHORD FINDER

AN EASY-TO-USE GUIDE TO OVER 1,100 GUITAR CHORDS
00697200 6" x 9" Edition $4.95
00697208 9" x 12" Edition $5.95

INCREDIBLE SCALE FINDER

AN EASY-TO-USE GUIDE TO OVER 1,300 GUITAR SCALES
00695568 6" x 9" Edition $4.95
00695490 9" x 12" Edition $5.95

Prices, contents and availability subject to change without notice.

FOR MORE INFORMATION,
SEE YOUR LOCAL MUSIC DEALER,
OR WRITE TO:

HAL•LEONARD®
CORPORATION
7777 W. BLUEMOUND RD. P.O. BOX 13819
MILWAUKEE, WISCONSIN 53213

www.halleonard.com   0706